ARRANBEE DOLLS

Identification
&
Value Guide

"THE DOLLS THAT SELL ON SIGHT."

Suzanne L. DeMillar
and
Dennis J. Brevik

COLLECTOR BOOKS
A Division of Schroeder Publishing Co., Inc.

Front cover: Dream Baby, Debu'teen, Nancy Lee

Back cover: Littlest Angel, Nancy

Cover design by Beth Summers
Book design by Joyce Cherry

COLLECTOR BOOKS
P.O. Box 3009
Paducah, Kentucky 42002-3009
www.collectorbooks.com

Copyright © 2004 Suzanne L. DeMillar & Dennis J. Brevik

All rights reserved. No part of this book may be reproduced, stored
in any retrieval system, or transmitted in any form, or by any means
including but not limited to electronic, mechanical, photocopy, recording,
or otherwise, without the written consent of the authors and publisher.

Searching For A Publisher?

We are always looking for people knowledgeable within their fields. If
you feel that there is a real need for a book on your collectible subject and
have a large comprehensive collection, contact Collector Books.

Contents

Nanette Bridesmaid.
See page 108.

Acknowledgments

This book on Arranbee dolls could not have been written without the generous support and contributions of many different people. Their enthusiasm for this project has given the authors added incentive and motivation to finish what has been a long and involved process. We sincerely wish we could have used all the photographs sent to us, and certainly wish to acknowledge all who have contributed either photographs or information on Arranbee dolls. Therefore, we extend our heartfelt thanks to:

Jackie Addington, Sharon T. Aikens, Ronda Andrews, Michelle Argomo, Cyndee Barlow, Elke Barrett, George Bassett, Earl Bethel, Sara Bernstein, Vivian Brady, Barbara Buch, Byerlys Doll Repair & Restoration, Millie Caliri, Theresa Carroll, Lynn Chambers, Kevin Colebank, Marge Cottone, Beverly Courtney, Deborah Crowley, Debbie Crume, Steve Crowthers, Judy Cullen, Judy Danalewich, Stephanie Dangerfield, Annette Davino, Andrea Davis, Mary Davis, Susan Davis, Delores Delgado, Frances DePaoli, Sherry Dent, Joan DiFiore, Joyce Eaves, Diana Eddy, Frances Edmonston, Delores Elliott, Francesca Ellis, Shirley Ellis, Dorothy Feingold, Mike Fournier, Susan Fowler, Jeanette Fuelling, Mary Furse, Mary Ann Gastiger, Paula Giany, Diana Gibson, Donna Giordano, Jeanne Glass, Jan Glaser, Martha Gragg, Lenore Grew, Sharon Griffiths, Nancy Gurney, Moira Hatton, Andrea Hooser, House of Windsor Antiques, Judith Izen, Carol Jacobs, Phyliss Janowski, Veronica Jochens, Judy Joyce, Ginger Kagarise, Jackie Krause, Teri Krug, Ida Labaki, Carol J. Lindeman, Marilee Lindgren, Theresa Lintz, Mike Lizarraga, Michelle Lopes, Margaret Ludwig, Lori Luke, Kristine Lundquist, Marionella's Dolls, Donnie Marsden, Karen Martin, Diane Martz, Carlene Masero, Susan Mason, Anita Maxwell, Sharon McDowell, Joanne McIntosh, Barbara McManus, Jeanne Melanson, Linda Melanson, Marge Meisinger, memories-by-the-bay.com, Shirley Merrill, Loren E. Miller, Nancy Miller, Sheryn Minton, Mary Miskowiec, Robert Modena, Jillian Montgomery, Lorene Moore, Suellen Musgrove, Beth Nelson, Tammi Nichols, Linda Nowariak, Michelle Otey, Linda Paschini, Donna Pauls, Steve and Laura Pestrisko, Sharron Powell, Stephanie Prince, Denise Rayburn, Patti Rhodes, Richard at Estates R Us, Betty Ross, Kathe Rossi, Daisy Saiger, Chris Sanders, Janet Schwartz, Marion Schmuhl, Kandie Silveira, Suzanne Silverthorn, Judy Simpson, Flora Smith, Hally Smith, Patricia Snyder, Lani Spencer-McCloskey, Nancy Splitstoser, Nancy Stark, Elliott Stein, Pam Strawn, Susan at Juliette's Garden, Ann Tardy, Angela Theisen, Kathleen Tornikoski, Nancy Van Neil, Sherri van Opijnen, George Wagner, Warren Wagner, Nancy Lee Walters, Peter and Portia Watkins, Dixie Wheeldon, Sue Wnek, Joan Willard, Dian Zillner, and Dominque Zima.

To Coty Dickson for her contribution of information on, and all the photographs of, Coty Girl;

To Marilyn McDonald for information on, and the majority of photographs of, Little Angel and Littlest Angel;

To Judith Izen for her information on Arranbee's history;

To Maria Weiskott, editor-in-chief of *Playthings* in New York City, for her kind permission to reproduce the magazine's editorials and photographs of the Arranbee doll company that were found in the magazine's archives, and to Constance Phifer for her untiring and generous assistance in helping us research the many heavy volumes;

To Linda Smith, President of Vogue Doll Company, Oakdale, California, for her review of our manuscript and enthusiastic response to our efforts;

To Shari McMasters and McMasters Doll Auctions of Cambridge, Ohio for kindly supplying us with photographs;

To Mary Ellen Smiley of the Wenham Museum, Wenham, Massachusetts, for all her efforts on our behalf in researching the museum archives, and for photographic support;

To Carol Sandler, Library Director at the Strong Museum, Rochester, New York, for her research of museum archives for Arranbee material;

And last, but not least, to two special friends, Christine Parcher and Sally McVey-Trueblood, for their constant support and encouragement, and their abiding faith in this undertaking.

About the Authors

Suzanne DeMillar was born in Providence, Rhode Island, one of four girls, and grew up in the little village of Pawtuxet Cove on Narragansett Bay. Suzanne's early life was filled with sailing and other water-based activities, in addition to art, music, and dance.

Suzanne's interest in dolls came early in life. At Christmastime, her mother and grandmother made doll clothes for every one of the four girls' dolls; Suzanne continued this tradition with her own daughters. Her mother was an artist and jewelry designer who taught at colleges in Vermont, Ohio, and Rhode Island. Her father was a consulting engineer; in the late 1930s, he designed the machine for a wire fabricating firm to make the knitted wire tubes which the Ideal Doll Company used for the arms and legs of its Flexy dolls. Suzanne's collection today includes the Flexy dolls, Sunny Sue and Sunny Sam.

A graduate of Connecticut State College, Suzanne sought artistic expression in several fields: music (she studied the harp at the Boston Conservatory), landscape painting, poetry (published in several volumes), and specialty clothing design, in addition to doll clothes design and doll collecting. Her concentration on dolls began in the mid-1980s when she learned professional doll repair and became a dealer in addition to enlarging her personal collection. Early in 1991, she met and married Dennis (Dan) Brevik. Together, they have been publishing an international mail order catalog for almost ten years, have their own web site (designed by Dan), and auction dolls frequently on internet auctions.

Dennis J. Brevik, "Dan," is a retired engineer. He has a degree in chemical engineering from the University of Detroit and became a rocket engineer more or less by accident. While working for Rocketdyne he conducted over a hundred static engine tests and was one of the design engineers of the F-1 thrust chamber, used on the Saturn V. He became enamored of computer software and switched fields, where he became known for his pioneering work on operating systems, database management systems, and programming languages. His interest in dolls developed as a by-product of his marriage to Ms. DeMillar. It was a case of sink or swim. He clearly remembers the first doll show he attended, where (he swears) there were a thousand dolls all beckoning him to come over and visit. Thus began his interest in dolls, particularly their design, production, and distribution. He also claims to have an eye for a pretty face, a quality which naturally drew him to Arranbee dolls.

Introduction

"The dolls that sell on sight." Arranbee first used this slogan in 1950 to aptly describe its dolls. From her own experience, Suzanne can verify the statement completely. When she was about twelve years old, having saved up both her babysitting money and her allowance, she set forth in pursuit of a goal. That goal? To buy her first doll on her own.

At a department store downtown, a counter displayed a large selection of dolls. Only one look and she immediately focused on one in particular: 17" Nannette, dressed in a blue striped dress and a tan pile coat with matching hat. This doll was so outstanding that she never really saw the others. Called a "walker," the doll had swing legs on a stuffed cloth body, with composition head and limbs. Suzanne had never seen anything like her before, and she claimed the doll as hers even before she handed the clerk her money. The memory of that very special doll and that very special moment in her life has inspired, in part, this book.

When we, the authors, announced our intention to write a book on Arranbee, we were met with immediate and widespread enthusiasm. Many, many collectors responded with information and photographs of Arranbee dolls in their collections. We could not use all the submitted photographs, but those we could are attributed. Unattributed photographs are by one of us (Brevik).

Since its beginning in 1919 and until it was purchased by Vogue Dolls in 1959, the Arranbee Doll Company produced a stunning variety of dolls. Arranbee dolls have been well loved by millions of children throughout the company's history, and currently enjoy a heightened popularity among doll collectors. To date, however, no specific book has been published on this company. References to Arranbee dolls appear in the majority of books on the general subject of dolls, but some of the information appearing in these volumes has merely been repeated from one doll book to the next, without verification from an original source. This book, therefore, is an attempt to bring together in one book all the information we have found through extensive research of a wide range of resources, a major one being the advertising done by Arranbee beginning in the early 1920s.

A note on pricing: the price accompanying an individual photograph in this book is either the actual selling price or that which was obtained at auction. Therefore, there will be a wide range of prices for similar dolls, and these will reflect the condition, popularity, maker, time of purchase, and area of the country where purchased. Taking into account all the variables of a secondary market, collectors should use the prices shown in this book as a guide only.

Any additions or corrections to this book about Arranbee dolls would be gratefully received. We can be reached through the publisher or through our website: www.demillar.com. If you have questions about pricing or identification, contact the author at the website mentioned.

Arranbee and Its Dolls
History of the Arranbee Doll Co.

When we first began this Arranbee book, we contacted Vogue Doll Company, the surviving company entity, who informed us that due to changes in ownership of Vogue Dolls, subsequent to the original acquisition of the Arranbee Doll Company, there were no archives extant that the current Vogue company knew about. Also, we were unable to find any surviving employees of Arranbee or descendants of the founder. However, through a stroke of good fortune, we discovered that Judith Izen had interviewed a Mr. Ernie Breiner shortly before his death in 1997, as part of her research on Ideal for her book *Collector's Guide to Ideal Dolls*. Mr. Breiner had been an employee of both Ideal and Arranbee. Ms. Izen's notes captured many of his recollections.

We have been able to partially reconstruct a history of Arranbee from Mr. Breiner's memories, from advertisements and articles in *Playthings* and other trade publications, and from surviving artifacts such as wrist tags, brochures, boxes, etc.

June 1922 advertisement from **Playthings.**

In two somewhat conflicting 1957 and 1958 *Playthings* articles, we found the genesis of the Arranbee Doll Company. It was founded in March 1919, just after the close of the Great War, with the intention of importing dolls and doll goods from Germany. The founder was 19-year-old William Rothstein (called Bill by his friends), a young man who was born in Poland in 1900, and immigrated to New York City with his family in 1909. The original location of the company was a Manhattan loft at 649 Broadway. Rothstein had at that time a partner named Berman, and according to Mr. Breiner, it was from the names Rothstein and Berman that the name Arranbee (R&B) derived.

The first three or so years of the company are very sparse on information: the first advertisement we found (*Playthings,* from June 1922) is one in which the outfit introduced itself as "Importers and Manufacturers Agents."

The emphasis in the early years was on imported German bisque dolls and doll supplies. They probably distributed American-made goods as well. A patent assignment in 1930 disclosed that Arranbee Doll Company was at that time a co-partnership between William Rothstein, his brother Morris, and Joseph Ardbaum. Morris' name first appears in an ad in 1926, while the first occurrence of Mr. Ardbaum's name was in this patent assignment.

What happened to Mr. Berman is not clear, but in those days partnerships came and went in the doll and toy business. Just when William's brother, Morris, joined the business is not known, and by 1938 his name disappears. As for Joseph Ardbaum, although he and Rothstein were associated until about 1947, we were unable to find any further information concerning him. By the late 1940s, Bill Rothstein had become sole owner.

In any event, over the years Rothstein became the principal figure in the company, and in many ways the history of Arranbee Doll Company must be intimately tied to his personality. We are convinced he must have been a very personable, energetic, likeable man with considerable insight into the doll business. The company was reasonably innovative, with a few patents and unusual offerings, but it was also know as a trend spotter. Rothstein also had a penchant for quality, and to this day Arranbee dolls and costumes are so noted.

The company's advertisement in the August 1922 *Playthings* (seen on this page) reveals the extent of the doll lines it carried. According to a 1960 article on the Arranbee Company in *Playthings*, Arranbee's most popular doll during the 1920s was My Dream Baby, an imported German bisque head doll manufactured by Armand Marseille. Within a few short years, as Arranbee became more established, these baby doll heads began appearing with the Arranbee name included, with markings such as "Germany/Arranbee." My Dream Baby appears to have been a competitor of the Bye-Lo baby dolls, another popular doll of the era.

As early as 1923, Arranbee was also selling bisque doll heads which were manufactured by Simon & Halbig, another German firm. These doll heads were different from Dream Baby and will be found marked "Simon & Halbig/Arranbee," some with a German patent number.

In early 1924, the company relocated to larger quarters at 5, 7, and 9 Union Square West, New York City. Its doll lines expanded further to include a selection of baby dolls called "Baby Character Dolls" and "Baby Sweater Dolls." Arranbee's mama dolls and fully jointed dolls also continued to be heavily advertised during this decade, as well as a full line of doll hospital supplies (including doll parts such as heads) and doll wigs.

August, 1922 advertisement in
Playthings.

April, 1922 advertisement in Playthings.

Another line the company carried was "bisque novelty dolls in sizes 4 to 10 inches with and without wigs and sleeping eyes." Since we have found no conclusive information on these little dolls, we can only surmise that they were what is know today as "all bisque" dolls and probably imported from Germany.

About 1925, Arranbee opened a manufacturing facility (thought to have been on Broadway), possibly because German economic conditions caused an unstable import market. They did not manufacture bisque heads and limbs, but instead went directly to composition. Also, in the summer of 1927, they moved their offices and showrooms to 894-900 Broadway.

September, 1924 advertisement in Playthings.

The decade of the 1930s was one of the most prolific in the company's history, despite the constraints of the Great Depression. This was the decade of Nancy and Debu'teen, two very popular dolls then and among the most desired Arranbee dolls today. By this time, too, Arranbee was receiving a well-deserved reputation for quality products at reasonable prices. Throughout the company's existence, they maintained this reputation and produced dolls of exceptional quality, with rare exceptions. Note the rather whimsical excerpt on the following page from a full page advertisement in the January 1931 *Playthings*.

In 1930, Arranbee was fortunate to acquire the services of Ruby Hopf as costume designer. Ms. Hopf was the sister of the celebrated Georgene Hopf Averill ("Madame" Georgene), designer of the Madame Hendron dolls. Ruby is responsible for the extensive and meticulous line of Arranbee clothing. She was with the company until the end in 1960.

In May 1931, Nancy first appeared in a *Playthings* advertisement.

The name Nancy (and its derivatives) was very popular with Arranbee, although the origin is not known. It was not the name of Rothstein's wife or any of his children, and he was too young to have grandchildren at the time. We suspect it was a catchy name meant to compete head-on with the popular Patsy doll that had been introduced a few years earlier. During the 1930s, the

January, 1931 advertisement in **Playthings.**

Probably Dream Baby composition heads. Photo courtesy of the Wenham Museum, Wenham, Massachusetts, donated to them by Virginia Graves Carlson of the Vogue Doll Company.

company produced four different composition dolls with the Nancy name, which are fully described in Chapter 5. Much like Dream Baby, Nancy was also a family name, and like the former, was carried over into the hard plastic and vinyl doll era with the Nancy Lee, Nancy Jane and Nanette named dolls. Arranbee also used one of its Nancy models for its line of small historical dolls in the late 1930s to early 1940s.

Here we should note that once Arranbee had found a popular doll name they tended to keep using it, with slight variations, for subsequent lines of dolls. Thus the names Nancy and Dream Baby are intimately associated with Arranbee throughout much of the company's history.

Arranbee and Vogue Dolls formed a commercial relationship in about 1927. By a stroke of good fortune, The Wenham Museum in Wenham, Massachusetts, has a series of slides contributed by Mrs. Virginia Graves Carlson, of the Vogue Doll Company, which undoubtedly are of Arranbee's composition manufacturing process. On the right are two of the pictures.

With the company expanding and prospering, an ultra-modern showroom was opened at the Fifth Avenue Building, 200 Fifth Avenue, in April 1938. This showroom was open until 1943 during the war, when Arranbee moved to 881 Broadway at the corner of 19th Street, and was reopened in 1951, when the company returned to the building.

Probably arms and legs for the cloth body of the Dream Baby. Photo courtesy of the Wenham Museum, Wenham, Massachusetts, donated to them by Virginia Graves Carlson of the Vogue Doll Company.

May, 1931 advertisement in Playthings with first mention of "Nancy."

In April 1938, there appeared in *Playthings* an Arranbee advertisement featuring "Cry Baby," an all rubber doll, as well as mentioning for the first time the so-called "Teen Dolls." Nanette is also listed in this advertisement for the first time; however, subsequent advertisements spell the name Nannette. Debu'Teen as a distinctly named doll was heavily promoted at the 1938 Toy Show in New York City. These latter two dolls, along with Nancy Lee, were popular Arranbee dolls of the composition era. The first Nannette was of the mama doll type, with a cloth body, and clothed in little girl dresses and pinafores. Nancy Lee was an all composition girl doll and today is often confused with Debu'teen; the later doll, however, has a slimmer

Photograph of the new Arranbee showroom, appearing in the April 1938 issue of Playthings. With the help of a magnifying glass, one can identify Dream Babies, Nannette Mama dolls, and Debu'teens.

face that appears slightly older. The wardrobe available for both Nancy Lee and Debu'teen included dresses, gowns with real fur jackets, and skiing and skating outfits.

A 1940 advertisement in *Playthings* establishes that the manufacturing facilities were then located at 881-887 Broadway.

Some of the composition Arranbee girl and baby dolls were continued into the early 1940s, but by then, a new medium for making dolls had been introduced — hard plastic. Dream Baby began appearing in hard plastic, but other dolls (such as Debu'Teen and Nancy) were not continued. Nancy Lee appeared in hard plastic as she had in composition; however, the hard plastic Nanette (with one *n*) was a different doll altogether, no longer a child but a true girl doll very similar to Nancy Lee. The outfits available for these two hard plastic girls were interchangeable and featured an extensive range of design and accessories, thanks to Ruby Hopf (see Chapters 6 through 9).

With the addition of the 12" Little Angel and 10½" Littlest Angel dolls in the early 1950s, Arranbee was prospering and needed representation on the West Coast, so from January of 1951 until Vogue took over the company, it had additional showroom space in the Western Merchandise Mart in San Francisco. The West Coast representative was Mr. Wesley R. Wetmore.

Little Angel and Littlest Angel were cute toddler-type dolls, and with their many and varied outfits were an immediate sellout; retailers across the country reported having a difficult time keeping up with the demand for them. Little Angel and Littlest Angel remain at the forefront of popular Arranbee dolls today (see Chapter 10).

By 1950, another new material, vinyl, was also heavily used for doll heads, arms, and legs, and either vinyl, or vinyl and cloth babies, toddlers, and mama dolls became quite popular, some having the Nancy and Angel names. Two mature-figured fashion-type dolls also appeared in vinyl — Coty Girl, a small fashion doll, and a larger fashion doll with a jointed waist and high-heeled feet similar to Ideal's Miss Revlon (both of which were produced for only a couple years; see Chapter 11). Arranbee's final vinyl dolls of the late 1950s were lighter in weight, reflecting the trend toward variations of vinyl and softer plastics and the decline of the use of hard plastic. These dolls are described in Chapter 12.

In 1955, the company opened a new manufacturing facility in Hicksville, Long Island, at 250 Duffy Avenue. This plant had 50,000 square feet and employed 300 people, with 108 sewing machines and a modern plastics division. Mr. Ernie Breiner set up the finishing line and managed it for three years. This is where the dolls were dressed, wigged, and packaged. Mssrs. Morris Goldberg and Virgil Kirby were each Production Managers, and Ms. Filicia Monestaro was Floor Manager. Having started with the firm in 1930, Ms. Ruby Hopf was now known as the "dean of doll fashion designers."

On November 23, 1957, William Rothstein died unexpectedly, leaving behind his widow, three daughters, three sisters, a brother, and six grandchildren. Four months later, in March 1958, Arranbee celebrated its 40th anniversary. An article, briefly outlining the company's history, appeared in the March edition of *Playthings*.

The March 1958 article also noted that a new president, Robert Wanderman, had been elected, and that Rose, William Rothstein's widow, was serving in an advisory capacity. Mr. Wanderman was William Rothstein's son-in-law, married to his daughter Alice. Another son-in-law, Jerry Lipsitz (married to Naomi), had become Vice-President. Mr. Henry Weisser had become Sales Manager. A third son-in-law, Michael K. Emerson (husband of Elaine), had been associated with the company from 1951 through 1954.

Following the founder's death, the family carried on the business for about a year, but ultimately sold out to Vogue Dolls. The Rothstein family dropped out of the business, and Mr. Weisser took over as Sales Manager of the Arranbee Doll Division of The Vogue Doll Company. Vogue then occupied the Fifth Avenue showroom with Arranbee as a division, using Arranbee molds until the Arranbee name was dropped in 1961. Since Arranbee had had a long association with Vogue (the early Toddles was a marked Arranbee doll), this seemed like a natural course. Although Vogue carried on several Arranbee dolls, Littlest Angel being one example, these ultimately became very different dolls (see Chapter 13).

Over the years, the Arranbee Doll Co. advertised extensively in *Playthings*, beginning in the very early 1920s. During 1950 and 1951, the company also advertised in national magazines such *Life* and *Women's Home Companion.* The November 24th, 1952 edition of Life magazine carried a special Toy Manufacturers Section in which Arranbee dolls appeared. The company's dolls also appeared in the following mail order catalogs: *The White House, Kohn Hochschild, Howland's, Gimbels, Ivey's of Asheville, Schuster's* and *Bamberger's*, as well as other retail store catalogs and trade publications.

A company is composed of people, many of whom we have already mentioned. For the sake of completeness we would also like to recognize these tireless salesmen who kept the dolls on the shelves and counters of America. They, too, played an important role. We list the remainder of the sales force in chronological order, noting the years in which their names appeared in ads in *Playthings*:

S. Frey	1926 – 1938
Charles Petlit	1929 – 1958
I.B. "Ickie" Schwartz	1947 – 1951
Max E. Clausen	1947
Joel Tasman	1954 – 1958
Perry Saftler	1954
Bob Liss	1958

Identification of Arranbee Dolls

Identifying Arranbee dolls can be confusing, especially since doll companies often bought whole dolls or parts from one another; Arranbee was no exception. As a result, faces of dolls from different manufacturers can be so similar as to defy identification. A good example is a ballerina doll from the 1940s, having the same face and floss wig as an Arranbee, that is distinctly marked A.C. (American Character). In addition, one of Madame Alexander's hard plastic Alice in Wonderland dolls bears a faint R&B mark. An Ideal doll was used for one of Arranbee's composition Nancy dolls; she is marked with an *x* in a circle on her head. To make it even more confusing, some of the same outfits worn by the *x* in a circle Nancy can be found on a marked Nancy doll. As for unmarked, nude Arranbee dolls, as with other doll companies, determining identity is a skill learned from studying and familiarizing oneself with known examples.

One of the dolls that Arranbee sold to another company was a 7" toddler with painted eyes. In the early-to-mid-1930s, Mrs. Graves of Vogue dolls bought these dolls from Arranbee to dress as Vogue's first Toddles doll. These dolls bear the words "Arranbee Doll Co." on their backs. This same doll was also used by Arranbee itself for a variety of characters. Sayco, among other companies, is known to have used a marked R&B model for one of their composition toddlers. In some case, the R&B name has been partially blotted out, but is still discernible with a magnifying glass. Additionally, Arranbee produced dolls without the company name (and packed in plain shipping cartons) for various mail order houses and retail stores.

Another example of Arranbee's association with other companies is found in an old advertisement in the April 1947 issue of *Playthings*. The half-page advertisement displays a picture of a Donald Duck pop-up toy in a tin box manufactured by the Spear Toy Co., stating that Donald was dressed by the Arranbee Doll Company.

The "Made in USA" mark appearing on the hard plastic Nancy Jane doll also appears on several other companies' dolls, Nancy Jane also has a similar face to Mary Hoyer, as well as to some of the hard plastic Vogue girls. Some of the Arranbee dolls marked Made in USA have R&B on the head. In the case of Nancy Jane, only the original clothes, tag, and suitcase could identify this doll correctly.

Wigs on Arranbee dolls can be found made of mohair and human hair on composition dolls, and a variety of synthetic hair on later ones, although human hair wigs were occasionally placed on the more expensive hard plastic girls. The company announced that it was the first to use the new material named "Dynel." Colors range from reds and browns to shades of blond; hair styles vary from casual flips to very elaborate French twists. Saran and nylon wigs were also used. The nylon wigs are not easy to style, and many have a stiff, unnaturally shiny appearance; hence, they are often found in braids. Before the advent of rooted hair, the vinyl headed dolls also had glued-on wigs. In the mid-1950s, an unusual feature of some Little Angel wigs was the appearance of colors not normally found in hair, such as green and red, an anomaly that was also found in other small dolls at the time.

Early eyes on the composition dolls were often painted onto the face. Prior to WW II, eyes were made of glass for the bisque head dolls, and metal with decal irises (some with a celluloid cover) for composition dolls. When metal was diverted to the war effort in early 1940, eyes were then made of glassene, which could shatter. Eye colors were either blue or brown, in a range of different shades. Although green eyes are sometimes seen, the color may actually be a blue which has faded or changed color over time. Since blue eyes were the preferred favorite on all dolls, Arranbee is unique for its extensive use of brown eyes.

Marks Found on Arranbee Dolls

Simon & Halbig/Arranbee, Patent Germany

Arranbee	R&B Doll Co.
R&B	Nancy
R&B on head, Made in USA on Back	Kewty
Nancy Made in USA (Nancy Jane)	P in a Circle (Coty Girl)
Dream Baby	Germany/Arranbee

In addition, the following numbers may appear, with or without R&B or Arranbee:

13	65
16	RB 76
17 BBS/RB/6 (BBS denotes models from other companies)	
18	210
23 ARV/R&B	250
49	283
59	341 or 351 with Germany (My Dream Baby)
63	620 with Germany/Arranbee
170	

Identification of Arranbee Doll Clothes

Arranbee doll clothes are exceptionally well made, with much attention to detail and design. There is also a tremendous variety in clothing style, including (but not limited to) ice skating dresses, ski suits, day dresses, and gowns, manufactured in a wide range of materials from cottons to silks. Fur jackets, some made of real fur, and fully lined with satin or the dress fabric, appear on both short dresses and evening gowns. The accessories that came with the dolls ranged from hats and bonnets to wristlets and scarves, with coordinating purses or parasols appearing with the more elaborate outfits. The bride dolls may also appear with small Bibles. Unfortunately, a common occurrence among all dolls is the loss of accessories over the years.

One of the main distinguishing features on Arranbee doll clothes for some of the composition and hard plastic dolls is the extensive use of narrow bias tape, or the dress material itself, for binding the edges of neck, sleeves, skirt hems, and back closures, some in an accent color to the garment. Following are several examples of this particular treatment:

Contrasting bias tape on the hem of Alice's dress.

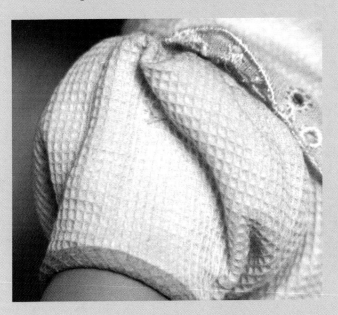

The sleeve edging is the same material as the dress but in a contrasting color. The mid-section of the sleeve is tacked to the top of the sleeve as a variation of the usual puffed sleeve.

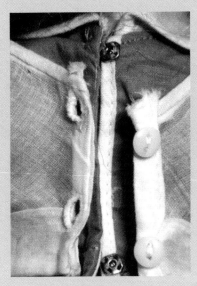

Back opening of Alice's dress and pinafore. Note that the pinafore uses buttons, while square snaps appear on the dress.

The dresses of many of the later hard plastic girl and toddler dolls have a simpler treatment of the back closure in that they open all the way down the back with the material simply folded along the edge and stitched. However, most have square snaps, which is another distinctive feature found on Arranbee clothing, although buttons can sometimes be seen on the back of the girls and baby clothing. Additionally, the sleeve edges may be simply folded under and gathered with lace. The dress in the first and second photographs above serves as an example of all of these features.

An unusual feature of Arranbee clothes on both the composition and hard plastic girl dolls is the addition of a fichu, either in the dress fabric or made of lace.

Undergarments on Arranbee dolls appear with the same attention to detail as outer garments, having bound edges and sometimes added decorations such as lace or bows. Fitted panties close with a snap or pin, while the bloomer style has an elasticized waist.

Some of the long slips also appear with attached pantalets and often have hoops in the hem or some kind of stiffening along the hem to give the gown a fuller appearance and to better display the costume and the material. The shorter dresses may have attached or separate half slips or panties.

Blue taffeta dress illustrating full-length opening without bias trim, with lace-edged, gathered sleeves.

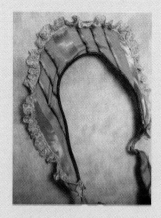

Self-fabric fichu on silk dress; it goes around the back of the neck to form a wide collar, crosses the bodice front, then ties in the back.

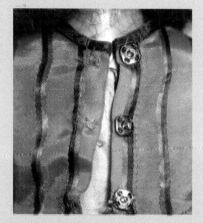

Silk dress on composition Nancy Lee showing bias trim neck and folded under edges of back opening that extend to just below the waist.

Lace fichu is attached with a button on the front bodice and pinned to back opening.

The shoes on Arranbee dolls were also given careful attention, with a variety of styles used. Of leatherette or oilcloth, they feature snap-front design, side-snap with cut-out designs, and composition child and baby shoes that tie. The girl doll shoes came in silver and gold, or were color matched to the individual outfits, although daytime clothes are often found with white snap or tie shoes. The white shoes may have the common, thin metal medallion as decoration. The Debu'teen doll's suede shoes, however, can sometimes be found with a flap over the front tie as a fashion accent. Saddle shoes in white and red, or white and brown, appear with suits or sporting outfits. Ice skates of gold, silver, or white are very realistic in appearance, with top stitching, separate tongue, and serrated blades. Arranbee's skis are also very realistic and were made of wood, with leather straps on the poles. While the skaters and skiers have appropriate winter attire, the roller skaters usually appear with day dresses! Plastic shoes appear on some of the 1950s dolls, mainly the high heeled shoes used for the fashion dolls. White predominates as the color for socks and stockings, which were manufactured of either rayon or cotton.

Where possible throughout this book, undergar-

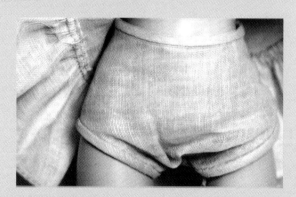

Fitted cotton panties having self-fabric binding on leg openings and waist. Full length slip is made of the same material.

ments and shoes have been photographed separately to show individual or unusual details. Wrist tags and box labels may occasionally be shown in an additional photograph, if they don't appear with the doll. Labels in Arranbee clothes are usually found on the named dolls such as Dream Baby, Nancy, Marianne, and Darling Daisy Bride.

When Arranbee first opened for business in 1919, the dolls and supplies they sold were both domestically produced and imported from Germany. The names of the earliest dolls are unknown, but since imported bisque head baby dolls were very popular with American families at the time, these were among the first to appear in the Arranbee line. One of the earliest Arranbee advertisements, found in *Playthings* of February 1923, reflected the uncertain times as the company appeared to be trying to reassure buyers that it was on top of the chaotic economic conditions in Germany.

By 1922, however, two bisque head baby dolls appeared with the name "My Dream Baby." Available with a closed or open mouth, they were manufactured by Armand Marseille, a well-known German company. The closed mouth My Dream Baby bore the number 341, while the open mouth version had number 351, both having Germany or A.M. with the number. There is a tremendous range of prices for these dolls due to differences in availability and the fact that many are not found with their clothes. There are not enough examples of some dolls shown to give a price range.

11½" DREAM BABY. Dome bisque head marked AM Germany 341. Composition gauntlet hands on one-piece stuffed cloth body with shaped legs (sometimes called a "frog" body). Rosy complexion and brown glass sleeping eyes; infant features and closed mouth. White organdy gown is accented with lace. Many of the bisque head dolls were sold nude, so it is not uncommon to find them redressed, as this one is.

Advertisement in **Playthings,** *February 1923.*

10½" MY DREAM BABY. Dome bisque head marked A.M Germany 351/10K. Five piece bent limb baby body. Open mouth with two bottom teeth. $250.00.

20" DREAM BABY. Fired black bisque head marked AM Germany. Open mouth showing two bottom teeth. Brown, bent limb composition baby body. Head has been repaired. $245.00.

Dream Baby & Other Bisque Head Dolls

As Arranbee became permanently established and needed dolls bearing its own name, these dolls began appearing with the Arranbee name or "Dream Baby" incised on the head. The registered trade mark for Arranbee's My Dream Baby, US. Pat. Office No. 202,243, was obtained in 1925.

It wasn't long, however, before Arranbee began designing and making its own dolls, many of which bore a distinct resemblance to the German bisque models. These new dolls were available with socket or shoulder heads, and came both dressed and undressed. In the remaining years of the Roaring Twenties, various new models of My Dream Baby (or simply Dream Baby) appeared with either bisque or composition heads.

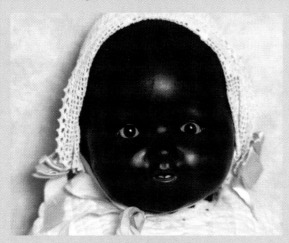

Head of 20" DREAM BABY.

14" ARRANBEE INFANT. Bisque head and composition arms, wearing antique clothes. $130.00. Courtesy of McMasters Doll Auctions.

14" DREAM BABY. Dome bisque head marked Germany/Arranbee. This is essentially the same mold as the AM doll, but it was made expressly for Arranbee. She has brown glass sleeping eyes. Cloth body is jointed at the hips, with a fat bottom so she can sit well; composition gauntlet hands. Baby gown has pink smocking; perhaps made just for her.

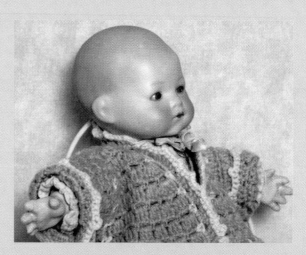

MY DREAM BABY. Marked Dream Baby on the head. Cloth body with composition hands has the same body as the preceding doll, but this one is stamped Mme. Hendron. Closed mouth, blue sleeping eyes. Redressed in white cotton gown and blue crocheted jacket. Sold for $165.00 in 2001.

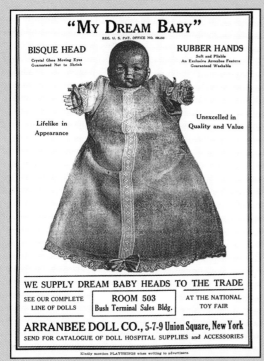

Advertisement for My Dream Baby from 1926.

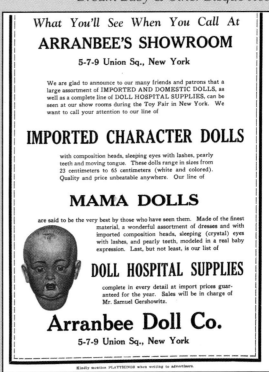

Further expansion in the mid-twenties saw Arranbee granting exclusive Canadian rights for its dolls to Lloyd Toy Co., as well as obtaining a license from Voices, Inc. for a patented voice box and crier for their new baby and mama dolls.

By the spring of 1923, the Arranbee line had expanded to include a 24" bisque head walking doll with a jointed body and a head that moved side to side with the walking mechanism; the doll also had "flirty" eyes.

May 1923 advertisement in Playthings. *The doll on the left, the "walking doll," has a bisque head, while the mama doll on the right has a composition one.*

Other bisque doll heads were imported from another German firm — Simon & Halbig. One such doll was a 28" girl with a kid body, composition limbs, and a head which appears to either be sprayed bisque or made of a material somewhere between bisque and composition,

called bisquique. The head on this doll is marked Simon & Halbig/Arranbee and Pat. #74720, which is not a US patent and is therefore most likely a Germany patent secured by Simon & Halbig in conjunction with Arranbee. Unfortunately, the photograph we have of this doll was not usable. A list of Arranbee patents and trademarks appears in Appendix II.

The advertisement above, from the January 1925 *Playthings* depicts an obviously bisque head with no reference to name or maker. Presumably, this head is a general representation of the bisque heads in the company's line.

June 1926 saw the introductory advertisement of the Nursing Bottle Baby, a new member of the Dream Baby family. This doll had a bisque head (a composition one soon followed) with composition and cloth or all composition bodies. The bisque head was incised Germany/Arranbee; the composition head was unmarked, but the Arranbee name was molded on the celluloid baby bottle. Both dolls had celluloid hands, the right one having the baby bottle permanently attached. When the hand was raised, the "milk" disappeared; when the hand was lowered, the "milk" flowed back into the bottle. Patent # 1,595,840 was issued on August 10th, 1926, for this feature. A version of Nursing Bottle Baby, known as Bottletot, had composition hands with a separate baby bottle. A full page ad in the September 1926 issue of *Playthings* ran a notice that the company had instituted suit in the Southern District Court of New York against another company for infringement on this patent. That same year, Arranbee advertised that it "supplied Dream Baby heads to the trade." (These two advertisement appear on the next page.)

THE ONLY PATENTED

NURSING BOTTLE BABY

This Doll
DRINKS MILK

Patent No.
1,595,840
Patented U. S
Patent Office
August 10,
1926

From an Unbreakable
Celluloid Bottle

The child simply raises the arm holding the
bottle to the doll's lips and the harmless
milk-like fluid bubblingly disappears. When
the arm is returned to its natural position,
the bottle magically refills.

Dressed in short and long Dresses
of the Finest Materials

*Bisque and
Composition Heads*
Exclusive Arranbee Models

The
ONLY Doll
of its type
you can buy
unhesitatingly
and with
genuine assurance
of protection.

IMMEDIATE DELIVERIES

NOTICE!

We hereby inform the trade that we have instituted suit in the UNITED STATES
DISTRICT COURT FOR THE SOUTHERN DISTRICT OF NEW YORK AGAINST
A DOLL MANUFACTURER for an injunction, damages and profits charging them with
infringement of United States Letters Patent No. 1,595,840, dated August 10th, 1926,
which we control. We hereby give notice to all doll manufacturers, jobbers, commission
houses and dealers that we shall protect our rights under this patent and are prepared to
institute suit wherever necessary to protect our rights.

ARRANBEE DOLL CO.
5-7-9 UNION SQUARE   NEW YORK CITY

Kindly mention PLAYTHINGS when writing to advertisers.

Advertisement for Nursing Bottle Baby in
Playthings, *1926.*

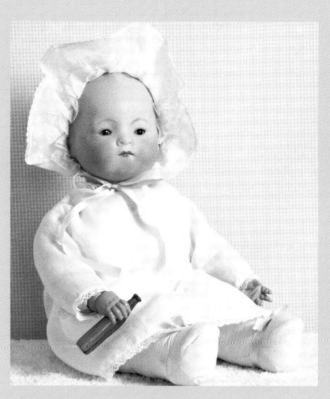

*16" NURSING BOTTLE BABY. Bisque head marked
Germany/Arranbee with spray-painted hair. Cellu-
loid hands with baby bottle attached to the right
one; cloth body has rather straight legs for a baby.
Vintage, white cotton baby gown and bonnet.
Sold for $110.00 in 2000.*

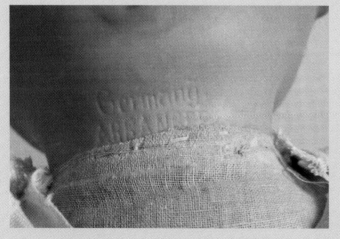

*Markings on head of 16" NURSING
BOTTLE BABY.*

"My Dream Baby"
With Bisque Head, Glass Moving Eyes and Rubber
Hands (An exclusive "Arranbee" feature)

*We supply "DREAM BABY"
heads to the trade*

DOLL HOSPITAL SUPPLIES
AND ACCESSORIES

WIGS, SHOULDER AND SOCKET HEADS,
EYES, HANDS, SHOES AND STOCKINGS, ETC.
SEND FOR ILLUSTRATED CATALOG
ARRANBEE DOLL CO.
5-7-9 UNION SQUARE   NEW YORK

January 1926 ad in **Playthings.**

Composition Babies and Toddleres

The late 1920's through the mid-1940's was a prolific time in Arranbee's history, with a variety of new dolls in composition or composition and cloth increasing the company's popularity. This time period saw the slow decline of imported dolls and a tremendous increase in production by American doll companies of composition dolls, composition being a more durable medium than bisque for doll heads. A 1926 advertisement in *Playthings* made note of the company's baby dolls having bisque or composition heads with "crystal eyes, pearly teeth, and a real baby expression." These new baby dolls were advertised extensively in trade publications with full-page descriptions and drawings, including several versions of My Dream Baby (or just Dream Baby) in several different sizes. The variations in the faces from a particular mold gave them an individual look not found in very many of today's mass-produced dolls. There is a tremendous range of prices for these dolls due to differences in availability and the fact that many are not found with their clothes. There are not enough examples of some dolls shown to give a price range.

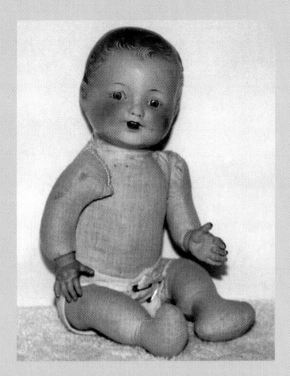

Body construction of 12" ARRANBEE BABY. The left hand fingers have melted, a common occurrence with rubber.

12" ARRANBEE BABY. Probably a Dream Baby; head is marked Arranbee. Separate molded tongue and molded teeth in open mouth; non-lashed metal sleeping eyes. Not original. $95.00.

ARRANBEE BABY. Facial detail of doll on the left.

23" DREAM BABY. All original, composition and cloth.
Lynn Chambers Collection.

19" DREAM BABY HEAD. Marked Dream Baby.
Body is in poor condition, but the head is in
good shape despite the eye crack. $35.00.

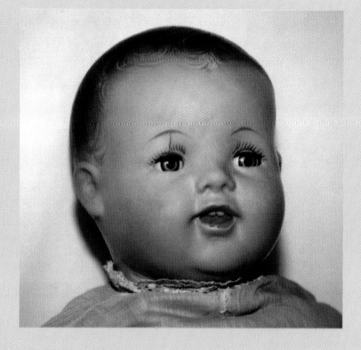

23" BABY DOLL. Marked Arranbee; may be another
version of Dream Baby. Composition and cloth with
exceptional facial modeling and real baby size.
Dressed as a boy in a white cotton knit, three-piece
outfit. He has also been called My Dolly, but this
name has not been verified. $245.00.

Another composition version of a bisque head doll was Bottletot, sometimes referred to as Bottle Tot. One of the following photographs shows the right hand molded in such a way as to hold a separate baby bottle, usually made of glass instead of celluloid.

The birth of the Dionne quintuplets in May 1934 lead to a new industry. Although the Madame Alexander Doll Company had a big winner with their exclusive rights to the Dionne name, Arranbee, like several other doll companies, produced unnamed versions of quints using a small, all-composition baby doll with a Dream Baby head. These dolls measure approximately 7", depending on the sitting or standing version.

In their January 1935 advertisement in *Playthings*, Arranbee spoke of a new, forthcoming doll: their "sensational novelty" was the "Drink'n Babe," and she truly proved to be a sensation. By the summer of that year, Arranbee's full page advertisements billed her as "The Outstanding Doll of the Year."

Drink'n Babe was obviously a very popular doll, judg-

7" DREAM BABIES. All are marked R&B and are original.
Millie Caliri Collection.

18" BOTTLETOT. Composition and cloth, with right hand molded to hold a baby bottle. All original.
Lynn Chambers Collection.

Arranbee's July 1935 advertisement in Playthings for DRINK'N BABE.

10" DRINK'N BABE. All composition, marked R&B. All composition with side-glancing painted eyes. Layette case holds accessories and original paper tag. Doll has hair repairs. $145.00.

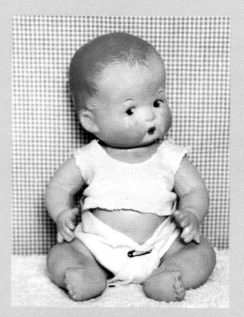

Full body of DRINK'N BABE.

Closeup of colorful graphics on inside lid of DRINK'N BABE case.

ing from her honor as being named one of the five most famous children of dolldom in 1936. The other dolls were: Shirley Temple, Happy Tot, Dionne Quintuplets, and DyDee Baby. Their photographs appeared in a special rotogravure section of the *World-Telegram* and other newspapers throughout the country. The following is an excerpt from the article in the December 1936 *Playthings*: "Last, but by no means least in our family of famous dolls, is Drink'n Babe, 'the doll that drinks like magic.' Drink'n Babe has enormous play value. It drinks milk naturally from a bottle so ingeniously constructed that it magically refills itself. Buyers all over the country state that its sales for the holiday season have been phenomenal."

By the autumn of 1936, Arranbee had added another novelty to its small baby line. Ink-U-Bator Baby was a "sweet-faced baby doll, packed in a sturdy incubator, the top of which contains a temperature dial and indicator,

as well as a cellophane covered observation window through which the little mother can observe the progress of the infant. The entire front of the box is also covered with cellophane. This striking replica of an incubator and baby is provided with an oxygen tube, rubber hot water bottle, stethoscope, nurses's cap, organdy dress, underwear, bonnet, knitted booties, blanket and pillow. The doll is dressed in a flannel diaper and knitted shirt" (Playthings, October 1936).

A few years later, Arranbee added another novelty, "A-Tisket, A-Tasket, A Dream Baby in a Basket," which was actually a variation of the small Dream Baby, and had sleeping eyes and molded hair. A full-page advertisement appearing in *Playthings* showed this doll in an elaborately decorated basket with matching coverlet and pillow and a complete layette. A carrying handle on the basket allowed a child to carry her doll with her. Without the basket, this particular doll cannot be identified properly.

INK-U-BATOR-BABY. Advertisement in October 1936 Playthings.

DREAM BABY in a BASKET. Advertisement in the September 1940 issue of Playthings.

7" DREAM BABY. All original, on coordinated pillow. This doll may actually be the Dream Baby in a Basket, but missing the basket.

What Arranbee advertised as a "Standing Baby" is called a "toddler" today. The majority of these appealing dolls have the Dream Baby head and are so marked. Made of all composition, they have realistic toddler shapes and cute baby expressions, molded hair, sleeping or painted eyes, and either open or closed mouths. The 11" size has a particular charm that has kept her popular over many decades, even without original clothes (as it is usually found today).

11" DREAM BABY. Marked on head and back. Blue sleeping eyes; open mouth showing two teeth and chin dimple. Original print dress over matching sunsuit. Cutout design on original blue Arranbee shoes.

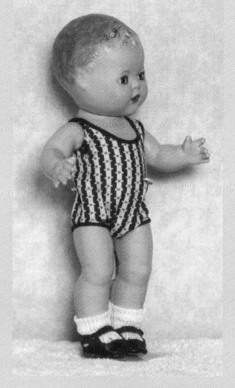

Sunsuit on 11" DREAM BABY.

13" DREAM BABY. All composition, 1927, marked Dream Baby. Vintage clothes. $135.00.

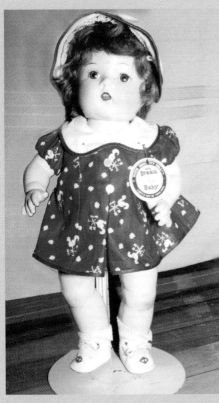

11" DREAM BABY. *Composition toddler marked Dream Baby on her back. Molded brown curls, brown eyes, open mouth showing two teeth and tongue. Not original. $141.00, internet auction.*

DREAM BABY. *Wigged version of preceding doll is all original with paper tag. No size given, but probably about 12".* Collection of Kathleen Tornikoski.

12" DREAM BABY TWINS. *Unmarked composition toddlers in matching, all original outfits. Head cracks have been repaired, otherwise dolls appear displayed only. This pair has been seen with Dream Baby markings. $295.00. If mint, this pair would be worth $450.00 and up.*

Back view of Twins.

Facial features of 12" DREAM BABY. Shown full length on previous page.

11" DREAM BABY. Marked with her name and having painted eyes. Original clothes and shoes, but her bonnet is missing. Appears displayed only. $195.00.

Closeup of 11" DREAM BABY showing her molded forehead curls.

Appearing in an August, 1940 advertisement, Little Angel was a new baby doll whose composition head resembled the bisque Dream Baby head. Having an expressive little face, and available in several sizes, she was one of Arranbee's "featherweight babies" and was described as a "Park Avenue doll, but at a popular price."

Her limbs were also made of composition, and her stuffed cloth torso concealed a crier. The design and execution of her dainty clothes was particularly outstanding for a war-time doll. Little Angel more than lived up to Arranbee's slogan, "The Quality Line at Popular Prices."

Doll Sales Soar Heavenward with
ARRANBEE'S LITTLE ANGEL

We also invite your inspection of our
FEATHERWEIGHT BABIES WITH ROLLING EYES

Dream Baby   Nancy Lee
Nancy   Nannette
Newly Created Doll Wardrobes
and Other Novelties
at our permanent showrooms:
ROOM 538
200 FIFTH AVE., N. Y. CITY

Not just another baby doll—rather a little bit of heaven that every little girl will want for her very own. Irresistibly appealing features combine with charming costumes to make "Little Angel" a doll personality that tugs at children's and parents' heart strings—and you know what that does to purse strings! And Remember, too, that Arranbee's popular price policy puts a smashing heavyweight sales punch behind this adorable featherweight doll.

ARRANBEE
DOLL COMPANY
Factory and Office: 881-887 Broadway, New York City

THE QUALITY LINE AT POPULAR PRICES

August 1940 advertisement for LITTLE ANGEL in Playthings. *First appearance of the LITTLE ANGEL name which continued on differing dolls for several years. See subsequent chapters.*

11" LITTLE ANGEL. Composition and cloth, with celluloid hands; brown eyes and closed mouth. Original dress and slip; bonnet and booties replaced. Marked R&B. $145.00.

Face of 11" LITTLE ANGEL.

17" LITTLE ANGEL. Larger version of previous doll with blue eyes. Not original. $110.00.

21" LITTLE ANGEL. Composition and cloth. All original. *Lynn Chambers Collection.*

17" LITTLE ANGEL. Composition and cloth. Red woolly snowsuit is trimmed with rabbit fur. Foil tag with her name. $125.00.

Although not made of composition, a doll which bears a likeness to the all composition Dream Baby doll is Cry Baby. An all rubber doll, she could drink from her bottle, wet her diaper, and cry real tears. The advertisement below from the April 1938 issue of *Playthings* carries an excellent picture of her, but no size is given. Unfortunately, no actual doll was found by the authors.

One of Arranbee's early and unusual little composition dolls was a 9" toddler with very curly, molded hair and side-glancing painted eyes. She carried the full company name, Arranbee Doll Co., on her back, with no markings on her head. Her distinctive body construction doesn't allow panties to be put on her. No information has been found on this doll, but with her deeply molded curls, she may possibly be Kurly Head, for which a trademark was obtained on March 17, 1930. She could also be another version of Nancy, of which there are several different models (many shown in the chapter on the various Nancy dolls).

Other dolls from this period found in other doll books, but not shown in this book, can be found in Appendix II at the end of the book.

Prices for Arranbee's composition babies and toddlers varied so widely in our survey that the individual prices shown with some of the previous photographs can only serve as a general guide.

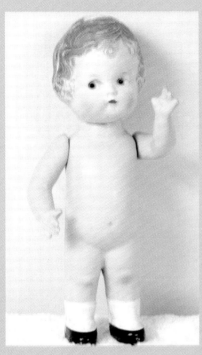

9" TODDLER. Photograph of body construction. Marked Arranbee Doll Co. on her back. $75.00.

Playthings *advertisement for CRY BABY, April 1938.*

9" TODDLER. This novelty doll may possibly be Kurly Head, a name that was registered by Arranbee in March of 1930, along with the Nancy name. Dress probably not orininal.

The two series of small dolls, "Around the World" and "Storybook Series," were produced from the late 1930's to the early 1940's. These 9" (can measure 8") composition dolls have molded hair and painted eyes, and are marked R&B Doll Co. The individually-designed presentation boxes they came in are decorated with colorful graphics depicting the characters from the story. In the case of nursery rhyme characters, the poem was also included on the inside cover. The boxes are true collectors items in their own right, as they reflect the artistic design of the period and are most delightfully executed.

Several sources have attributed the model for Arranbee's small composition dolls to Carolyn Lee, the five-year-old child movie star of 1939 through 1941. Born in 1935, she made only four movies in her short career before her parents took her away from Hollywood. Perhaps most notable of her movies was Birth of the Blues in 1941 in which Bing Crosby sang her to sleep with "Melancholy Baby," the number one hit song that year.

An interesting note on the Snow White doll: she was originally called "Snow Drop." She had blond hair and blue painted eyes, and Arranbee dressed her in a white cotton gown and a pink cape. This doll appeared prior to the Walt Disney movie; in the movie, however, this char-

actor became Snow White and her hair color was changed to black. The bright primary colors on the clothes in this movie became the traditional ones associated with Snow White today. Snow White can therefore be found in several different hair and costume color combinations, all of which are original and show the gradual evolution of Snow Drop to the traditional Snow White.

Other dolls known in the two series, but not photographed here, include Jack and Jill, Little Boy Blue, and a Sailor Boy. Prices for dolls in these two series range from $65.00 for played with and not original to $395.00+ for original dolls in original presentation boxes.

One little 8" storybook-type boy, whose photograph appears near the end of this chapter, is a mystery. All composition, and distinctly different from the above dolls, he is marked R&B but looks just like Vogue's Toddles. However, he does not appear in *Collector's Encyclopedia of Vogue Dolls* by Judy Izen and Carol Stover. Whether an international or a storybook doll, he is quite unique with his yellow yarn hair and original, brightly colored clothes. Hopefully, more information on this little doll will come to light as collectors become more familiar with Arranbee dolls.

9" BO PEEP. All original with 3 lambs. $155.00 at auction in 2000. **Collection McMaster's Doll Auctions.**

9" SNOW DROP or SNOW WHITE. Marked Arranbee Doll Co. All original.

9" SNOWDROP. *This one has blond hair. She is all original, in a colorful box with the dwarfs printed on the inner lid.* Sara Bernstein Collection.

Inside cover of original box for 9" SNOWDROP.
Sara Bernstein Collection.

9" SNOW WHITE. *Marked R&B. Black hair, brown painted eyes. Traditional colors on outfit. All original.* $145.00.

9" COWGIRL and COWBOY. *All original, but probably wore hats.* $225.00.

9" PIRATE. All original.
Millie Caliri Collection.

9" MARY HAD A LITTLE LAMB. Original red check dress and bonnet. Lace on bodice is replaced; shoes are not original.

9" ARRANBEE DUTCH BOY. Marked R&B on back. Original outfit (except cap); wooden shoes are nailed to his feet. Repair on top of head.

9" R&B DUTCH GIRL. Original clothes; her wooden shoes are missing.

Pair of DUTCH CHILDREN. Girl's wooden shoes are replacements, but are a good match to the boy's.

8" CHARACTER BOY. Marked R&B, painted features. Original, but unknown outfit appears to be a storybook character. The pants and hat are made of felt; the shoes are not original.

Composition Nancy Dolls

Nancy was, by far, Arranbee's most popular name. Appearing first in 1931, the Nancy name, or variations thereof, was carried by a number of dolls well into the 1950's; however, the many versions of the Nancy-named dolls bear little or no resemblance to one another. The trademark for the Nancy name, as well as for an unknown doll named Kurly Head, was registered on March 17, 1930.

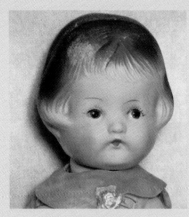

Facial features of 14" NANCY, marked Kewty. Painted eyes.

Same doll as in upper left photo, but having metal sleeping eyes.

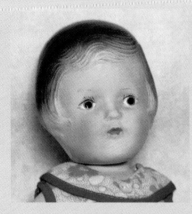

Facial features of 12" Marked NANCY.

Facial features of 16" Marked NANCY.

Facial features of 11" NANCY, marked Arranbee.

The earliest Nancy dolls were either made of all composition or with composition head and limbs on a stuffed cloth torso. Since most of the composition Nancy dolls were produced from the 1930's to early 1940's, it is difficult to ascertain which was actually the first version. Advertisements from that era list only "Nancy" and "Nancy Novelty Dolls," without accompanying photographs or illustrations.

To begin with, a 14" composition Nancy was actually an undressed doll purchased by Arranbee from another company. She had molded bobbed hair with bangs, so typical of the period, and either painted on or metal sleeping eyes. Her chubby body was that of little girl of about five or six years old. "Kewty" appeared on her back in raised letters, but her clothes and wrist tag pro-

claimed her name to be Nancy. She is sometimes confused with another doll marked Kewty which bears no resemblance to her. Arranbee dressed her in the usual high-waisted little girl dresses of the period. She was also available in a trunk with a wardrobe of various outfits. The wardrobe trunk was made of wood, had space for the doll, and contained not only a clothes rod and hangers, but drawers to carry shoes and accessories. The diamond-shaped sticker on the trunk proclaimed that it was "Nancy's Wardrobe;" her clothes carried labels with the Nancy name on them. With a bent right arm, also, she had as much charm as Effanbee's "Patsy," of whom she appears to have been a competitor. Less often found today than other Nancy dolls, she is a collector's prize.

13" NANCY. All composition, marked Kewty on her back. Painted blue eyes and orange hair. All original, with Nancy label on dress.

13" NANCY. Same doll as preceding one, but having metal sleeping eyes. Appropriate redressing. Seam repair on top of head. $155.00.

13" NANCY, using the marked Kewty doll. Wardrobe trunk carries a "Nancy's Wardrobe" sticker. Roller skates and extra play wear included.
Courtesy of Sharon T. Aikens.

13" NANCY. Same as the preceding doll set, including sticker, but in a red trunk with different outfits.

Another Arranbee Nancy was a 12" doll bearing her own name on her back. This all composition model had painted blue eyes and light brown, molded hair that was parted on the side, with a wave across the forehead rather than bangs. A slimmer doll than the Kewty model, she appeared to be a slightly older child, even though she was smaller. Her right arm was also bent, which was typical of the early Nancy's as well as similar dolls of the period. Generally, her features were not quite as striking as the Kewty model, but her size and childish appeal made her a popular doll. She, too, came in a variety of period-style dresses, most with matching shirt/panties combination and bonnet, and was also available in a trunk. The trunk carried the same sticker as the preceding doll.

An 11" version was marked Arranbee, with her wrist tag stating her name as Nancy. She had painted, side-glancing eyes and her face was exceptionally cute, with an impish expression. Her hair was an orange-brown in color, with deeply molded waves and a molded loop on the right side to which a hair ribbon could be tied. None of the other Nancy dolls had this unusual feature. Like the Kewty model, she is not commonly found today. A black version of this particular model had very distinct, heart-shaped painted black eyes; she has been referred to as "Sweetie Lue," but this name has not been verified in an original source.

12" NANCY. Composition, marked Arranbee Doll Co. Original coat and cap. $140.00.

12" NANCY. Marked Arranbee Doll Co. Original print dress, rest of clothes replaced.

12" NANCY. Wardrobe trunk has "Nancy's Wardrobe" sticker. Outfit she wears has a Nancy label. Trunk outfits are also original, with the sailor dress having a label. $225.00.

Extra clothes in trunk.

11" NANCY. Arranbee Doll Co. on back. Molded hair loop to hold bow. Original and in excellent condition. $325.00.

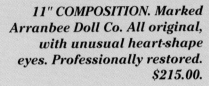

11" COMPOSITION. Marked Arranbee Doll Co. All original, with unusual heart-shape eyes. Professionally restored. $215.00.

11" NANCY. Original dress and matching bonnet. Not in good condition. $58.00.

12" BOY. This is the same doll as the preceding one, but without the molded loop. Original pink shorts and print shirt; oilcloth shoes are old replacements. Marked Arranbee.

Still another Nancy model had an open mouth, full cheeks, and a mohair or human hair wig in various colors. She can be found marked Nancy, Arranbee, or with no marks at all. She came in several sizes, from 16" on up, and was available in either all composition or in composition and cloth, the later doll also available with molded hair. The earliest eyes on these Nancy's were blue metal, but later models had glassene eyes in various shades of blue or brown. The variety of her clothing was extensive, featuring simple, little girl dresses to very detailed gowns, some of which came with real rabbit fur jackets. The quality of the clothes was exceptional, and much attention was given to her underclothes, as well. As with other Nancy models, the Nancy label often appeared on her clothes. Popular when first produced, she remains a much sought-after doll today.

16" NANCY the NURSE. Cap is missing, otherwise all original. Never played with. $382.00 in a 2001 internet auction.
Anita Maxwell Collection.

17" NANCY. Golden curls and original yellow organdy dress, shoes, and socks. **Millie Caliri Collection.**

18" PRINCESS NANCY. All composition, marked Nancy. Human hair wig. Yellow taffeta gown, gold snap shoes with medallion, panties attached to slip. Crown is a replacement. $200.00, 2001.

Closeup of 16" Nancy.

16" NANCY. Marked Nancy. Mohair braids, brown eyes. Organdy pinafore, matching romper, oilcloth shoes. Clothes are original; blue straw hat is a perfect replacement. $285.00.

20" NANCY. Composition and cloth, with swivel head on shoulder plate, marked Arranbee. Brunette wig and sleeping eyes. All original in pink. Sold for $215.00 in 1998.

20" CHILD. Same construction as preceding doll, but molded hair gives her a different look. May also be a Nancy, but she has been called "Rosie" in several books (no original source for this name has been found). Doll has been restored, but is all original.

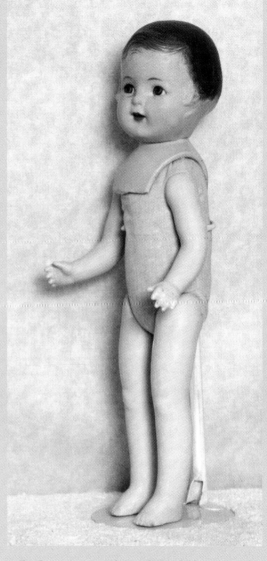

Body construction of the 20" marked Arranbee doll.

19" NANCY. Marked Nancy composition swivel head; composition limbs on cloth body. Original yellow organdy dress and shoes; human hair wig in long curls. Sold for $225.00 in 1999. Unknown doll on right.

17" PRINCESS NANCY. *Another version of the Princess, with a gold crown.*

17" PRINCESS NANCY. *Pink taffeta gown, matching handbag, silver crown, and replaced shoes. Unmarked and may actually be an Alexander doll; however, the dress has a typical Arranbee detail - crossed fichu on the bodice.*

14" NANCY. *All original, marked with an x in a circle on her head. Purchased nude from another company and dressed by Arranbee. Brown braids and eyes. Sold for $220.00 in 1999.*

18" NANCY. *All composition, marked with her name. Human hair wig, dark blue eyes. Original pink silk dress has smocked bodice. A much younger appearance on this Nancy. Sold for $195.00 in 1999.*

17" NANCY. Original blue dress has smocked bodice and matching cap. Shoes are not original.
Marilee Lindgren Collection.

16" NANCY. Sold for $300.00 in 1996.
Courtesy McMasters Doll Auctions.

17" NANCY. Several variations of this design will be found on other Nancy dolls. This one has a taffeta bodice, with a large bow detail on the back. Original except for the bonnet.

Rear view of preceding 17" Nancy.

14" NANCY. All composition, marked with an x in a circle. Golden brown wig and brown eyes. Original throughout. Note her matching, basket-shaped bag.
Marilee Lindgren Collection.

19" NANCY. All composition, marked Nancy. Silver crown pin has "jewels," and the doll is thought to be in recognition of Elizabeth when she became heir to England's throne in 1936. All original. $250.00.
Courtesy of Flora Smith.

15" NANCY. This is a smaller version of the preceding doll; marked with the x in a circle. All original, with same silver crown pin. $275.00 in 2000.

Facial study of 15" NANCY showing silver crown pin with "jewels."

17" NANCY. Marked Nancy. Blond mohair wig, light blue eyes. All original, including pink oilcloth shoes. Sold for $275.00 in 1998.

16" NANCY. All composition, marked Nancy. Brunette wig, bright blue eyes. Original pink organdy gown; slip has attached pantalets. White tie shoes.

17" NANCY. Blond wig and brown eyes. Organdy gown and picture hat, all original. Marilee Lindgren Collection.

17" NANCY. Golden blond wig and brown eyes. All original, variation of preceding doll.
Millie Caliri Collection.

15" NANCY. Unmarked, all composition, with blue tin eyes and blond curls. All original, in blue organdy petal dress and matching undies and wearing oil-cloth shoes with medallions. Original, shield-shaped tag denotes an early 1930's doll. Dress has shelf soil. $450.00.

Rear view of 15" NANCY.

13" NANCY. *Unmarked girl similar to preceding doll, but having an open mouth. This dress, in different colors, can be found on Debu'teen. This doll also has extra Arranbee clothes. $235.00.*

Closeup of facial features of 13" NANCY.

22" NANCY. *Composition and cloth, with human hair wig. All original, in green organdy dress, with shield tag.* Marilee Lindgren Collection.

20" NANCY. *All composition, marked Nancy. Green velvet coat and hat trimmed with rabbit fur are copies of original; oilcloth shoes. Sold for $195.00 in 1999.*

In the early 1930's, a 12" Nancy doll was used for an historical series of dolls entitled Cherrie Historical Dolls. The clothes had Nancy labels, but the dolls were not known by that name. The George and Martha Washington set of dolls was typical of this series. Their white wigs were actually powdered, and their clothes authentically detailed. This pair was presented in 1932 at Mount Vernon for the commemoration of the 200th anniversary of George Washington's birth. The George doll was particularly notable, as he sold exceptionally well for a boy doll.

In addition to the historical doll series, an international set was also available. The same attention to detail appeared in this series also, with the Dutch girl actually having wooden shoes. Her unusual red and gold wrist tag has the R&B logo and her name, Duchess Nancy. Acquired from another doll company, she is marked with only the number 13 on her back. She has very yellow braids and an open mouth, and her complete outfit is of typical Dutch design. These dolls were issued about 1938 – 1939, most likely in order to coincide with the 1939 New York World's Fair.

Price range on Nancy dolls: $75.00 for fair to good condition; $150.00 to $500.00+ for mint dolls.

12" GEORGE AND MARTHA WASHINGTON. Cherrie Historical Dolls series. All composition, marked Arranbee Doll Co., with original boxes. George Washington print on the dress with the dates 1732 and 1776. 1932 commemoration of the two hundredth anniversary of George Washington's birthday.
Courtesy of McMasters Doll Auctions.

12" MARTHA WASHINGTON. All original.

13" DUCHESS NANCY. *Marked only 13, but wrist tag bears her name. Open mouth, bright yellow mohair braids. Original except for replaced Dutch bonnet and flag. Blue dress with pink velvet bodice is quite faded, wooden shoes are nailed on. An 'attic' doll with some restoration. $260.00.*

Closeup of Duchess Nancy wrist tag.

Composition Debu'teen

and Other Teen Dolls

In 1938, Arranbee entered a distinctly new phase with its "Teen Dolls," the first of the slim, teenage dolls. After its initial advertisement, the company thereafter carried only the name Debu'teen in its advertisements. Promoted as the "teen fashion of her era," she was available in several sizes up to 22". This older girl doll was produced in either all composition or with a composition head on a shoulderplate, composition limbs, and stuffed cloth torso. The legs on the latter dolls were attached at the sides so they could stand, unlike the swing legs of the Nannette Mama doll. The following is an excerpt from the announcement of Debu'Teen dolls in the July, 1938 issue of *Playthings*:

"Arranbee Doll Company ..... featuring 'Debu'Teen Dolls,' a newly designed line that typifies the 'teen age of girlhood. The refreshing sub-deb facial expressions are enhanced by attractive modern coiffeurs. A wide variety of costumes, representing both sport and formal styles, follow the prevailing trend in present day teen age design."

Debu'teen Facial Features

The Debu'teen face is generally that of an older girl, with a slightly more mature and thoughtful expression than either Nancy or Nancy Lee. Although she is occasionally confused with Nancy Lee, a careful study and familiarization with her face will make her readily recognizable as the distinct doll she is.

Closeup of 13" DEBU'TEEN. All composition, marked R&B.

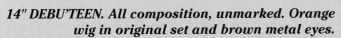

14" DEBU'TEEN. All composition, unmarked. Orange wig in original set and brown metal eyes.

Facial features of 17" DEBU'TEEN. This the familiar Debu'teen "look."

17" DEBU'TEEN. Composition and cloth, marked R&B. Very blond human hair wig and dark blue eyes.

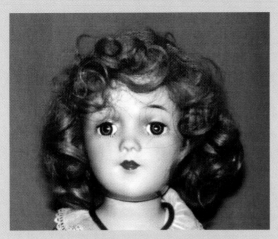

20" DEBU'TEEN marked R&B.

22" DEBU'TEEN. Composition and cloth, marked R&B. Large dark eyes and reddish blond wig give her a very appealing face.

Closeup of the 22" DEBU'TEEN having bent legs. Full photograph shown on page 61.

Typically, the larger Debu'teen dolls have human hair wigs, with mohair mostly on the smaller sizes. On both, the wig is parted on the side, with graceful waves or curls as befitting an older girl. Eye colors cover a range of shades from blue to brown, the earliest eyes being made of metal; later Debu'teens, however, have glassene eyes. Most of these teen dolls are marked R&B and were available with an extensive wardrobe ranging from sporting outfits to lavish gowns with real fur jackets. The Debu'teen name was not continued in hard plastic, and does not appear in advertisements after 1940.

It should be noted that some of the Debu'teen dolls in sporting outfits resemble the Vogue Sporting Women Series of the 1940's. Debu'teen is generally marked R&B, but the Vogue versions usually are unmarked. It is possible that Vogue bought unmarked nude dolls from Arranbee, as there are striking similarities in both the faces of these dolls and their various outfits. In addition, the Vogue dolls appeared after the advertisements for Debu'teen ceased.

> Prices for Debu'teen dolls:
>
> Original gowns (higher amount reflects doll with fur jacket and/or tag): $250.00 – 650.00+.
> Partially original in street outfits: $125.00 – 250.00.
> Played with and not original: $65.00+.

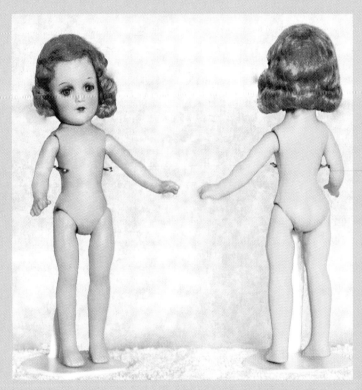

14" DEBU'TEEN. Front and back view of all composition version, marked R&B on her head.

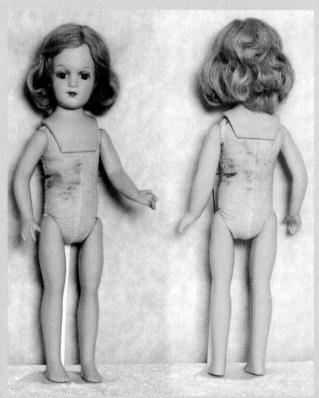

17" DEBU'TEEN. Body construction of composition and cloth model, showing front and back. The head is marked R&B.

22" DEBU'TEEN. Detail of body construction. Head is not marked, but legs or arms may be found with R&B hidden by the joint.
Anita Maxwell Collection.

17" DEBU'TEEN. Composition, 1938. Plaid dress and jacket, felt hat, suede shoes. Blond human hair wig, brown sleep eyes. All original. $375.00.

This photograph shows the dress without the jacket on the 17" DEBU'TEEN.

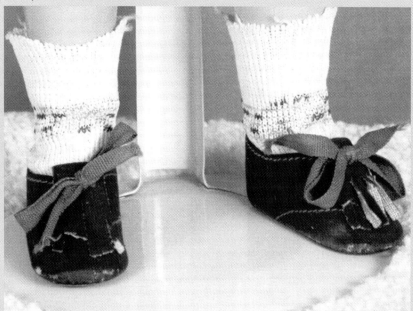

Unusual suede shoes on 17" DEBU'TEEN.

17" DEBU'TEEN. All original, with tag. $225.00, 1997 auction. Courtesy of McMasters Doll Auctions.

20" DEBU'TEEN. Composition and cloth, 1938. Auburn mohair wig, brown eyes. Light brown organdy dress, all original. $285.00.

13" R&B DEBU'TEEN RIDER. Carrot-red mohair wig and dark blue sleeping eyes. Original riding outfit, box, and paper tag. $400.00, 1996 auction. *Courtesy of McMasters Doll Auctions.*

13" DEBU'TEEN RIDER. Unmarked, all composition, in original riding outfit and shoes. This is the only Debu'teen the authors found having painted eyes. She resembles the Dream Dolls, and may have been purchased nude and dressed by Arranbee, but the authors have seen her with her original wrist tag.

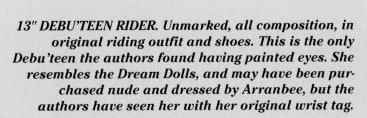

TRIO of DEBU'TEENS. Sizes 18" and 20" are marked R&B; size 23" unmarked. All are original.
Anita Maxwell Collection.

11" DEBU'TEEN SKIER. All original, composition. Originally came with Debu'teen tag.
Photo by Judith Izen, from the Marion Schmuhl Collection.

18" R&B WAVE in SUITCASE. Composition and cloth Debu'teen. Human hair wig, green eyes. Red metal trunk holds extra clothes. $395.00.

Full length of WAVE showing dress.

13" DEBU'TEEN. Marked R&B on head. Original blue jumper and blouse; missing felt hat. Blue tin eyes and mohair wig. $135.00 in 2000.

17" R&B WAC DOLL. Composition. All original, with wrist tag. Sold for $330.00 in 1996 auction.
Courtesy McMaster Doll Auctions.

18" DEBU'TEEN. Composition swivel shoulderhead, 1938. Dark golden brown human hair wig and brown eyes. Original red dotted jumper with separate blouse is a color variation of the preceding dolls. Straw hat and shoes are not original. $195.00.

18" DEBU'TEEN. Composition and cloth girl marked R&B on head and limbs. This is a typical Debu'teen outfit with ghillie type shoes. Brunette, human hair wig. Cap is a different material from jacket, but brass button matches those on jacket. $385.00.

17" DEBU'TEEN. Composition and cloth. Human hair wig and greenish eyes. Original plaid skirt attached to camisole top and tan jacket. Cap, shoes, and socks not original. 2000 online auction, $178.00.

17" DEBU'TEEN. Underclothes and gold shoes on this doll are original, indicating that she was originally dressed in a gown.

SKATING PAIR. Both are marked R&B. Original, with almost identical outfits. Anita Maxwell Collection.

17" DEBU'TEEN. Very fashionable outfit with real fur jacket — an exceptionally high-quality, expensive doll. This outfit also came in green. Patricia Vaillancourt Collection.

14" PRINCESS BETTY ROSE. All original Debu'teen doll in original box marked #3790. Real fur jacket marks her as an expensive doll.
Marilee Lindgreen Collection.

14" DEBU'TEEN. Blond human hair wig. Blue suit and hat, real fur jacket. All original, with name tag. Evidently an expensive doll when she first appeared, she remains highly prized by collectors today.
Marilee Lindgren Collection.

17" DEBU'TEEN. Blond human hair wig. Unidentified outfit is carefully coordinated.

Seated Debu'teen

An unusual version of the composition and cloth Debu'teen can be found with slightly bent legs. This particular feature allows the doll to sit gracefully, but makes her appear awkward standing up on a doll stand. She has the distinctly Debu'teen face and upper body, and has been found only in the 22" size. Because she is unmarked and the known examples appear without original clothes, she remains a mystery.

22" DEBU'TEEN. The face on this seated girl is a bit more pensive than the straight leg version. She is unmarked, and has been appropriately redressed in old princess-style dress. Eagerly sought by collectors, she remains an elusive doll.

22" DEBU'TEEN. Unmarked, with bent legs. Unlike the larger size Debu'teens, the bent leg versions appear with mohair wigs. This one is blond; eyes are dark blue. The early 1900's sailor outfit suits her well, but is not original.

Nude view of the 22" bent-leg version of DEBU'TEEN.

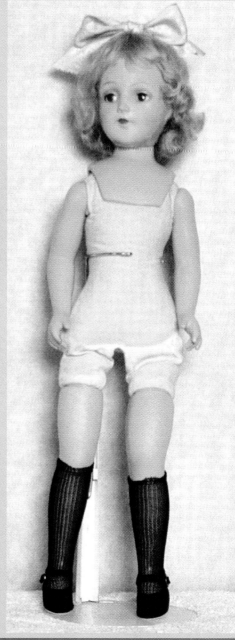

Body construction of the 22" DEBU'TEEN. She looks awkward posed like this. Her upper half is the same construction as the straight leg model, but her hips and legs are constructed like a Dresser or Bed Doll.

Rosalie

Another mystery doll among the teenage group is Rosalie. She was advertised in the Sears Christmas catalog for 1939 and billed as the American Girl, but her face and description are distinctly Debu'teen's. The advertisement states that she was available in three sizes, with a human hair wig on the larger sizes, and a wig of mohair on the smallest. The Rosalie name is not found in other advertisements in the authors' collection, so she may have been a special doll created just for the Sears Christmas market; however, since (with rare exceptions) Sears did not mention the manufacturers of its dolls, no attribution to Arranbee was given. Found marked or unmarked, Rosalie is, indeed, a rare doll.

New "Rosalie"
THE AMERICAN GIRL
$1.98
13½-In.

- **Beautiful Go-To-Sleep Eyes.** ● **Turning Tilting Head**

The New gorgeous teen-age doll that has captured the heart of every one. She's slender, chic, and natural—a perfect symbol of this streamlined age. Inside washer jointed arms and legs, long, slim and graceful with sparkling, glass-like eyes, real lashes. Dressed to the minute in dotted, pleated, flared organdy dress with bolero, artificial leather belt; cotton duvetyn poke bonnet with ribbon chin strap, white undies; roll top rayon socks; white snap buckle, artificial leather shoes.

49 V 3360—13½-In. Mohair Wig. Shpg. wt., 1 lb. 4 oz. $1.98
49 V 3361—18 - In. Real Human Hair. Shpg. wt., 1 lb. 8 oz. . .2.98
79 V 3363—24 - In. Real Human Hair. Shpg. wt., 3 lbs. 4.98

Advertisement in the 1939 Sears catalog for ROSALIE.
From the collection of Marge Meisinger;
photograph by Suzanne Silverthorn.

13" ROSALIE. Marked R&B, all composition, with brunette wig and brown eyes. Original organdy, dotted brown dress; separate yellow cotton bolero is trimmed in brown. Original slip/panties combination and leatherette shoes with medallion. The belt and bonnet are replacements. This doll is featured in the preceding advertisement.

"Rosalie"—Teen-Age Doll

$1.98

- Shadowed sleeping glass-like eyes.
- Turning, tilting head. • Long lashes.

"Rosalie" is 18 in. tall and just the right age to wear grownup clothes! For her Christmas morning debut, she chooses a swing style dress and red felt hat. White undies, lacy slip—socks—tied buckle shoes. Slim, all composition doll—human hair ringlet wig—inside jointed arms and legs.

49 V 3326—Shpg. wt., 1 lb. 12 oz. ... $1.98

Advertisement in 1939 Sears catalog showing ROS-ALIE. This Christmas outfit features a white dress with a red hat. From the collection of Marge Meisinger; photograph by Suzanne Silverthorn.

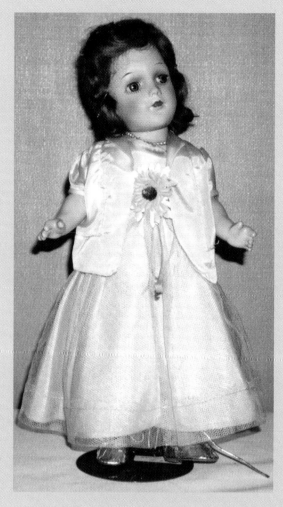

17" TEEN DOLL. Resembles Rosalie, but she has a composition swivel head, cloth body, and composition limbs. Original yellow tulle over taffeta gown, with short sleeve jacket and gold evening shoes. Millie Caliri Collection.

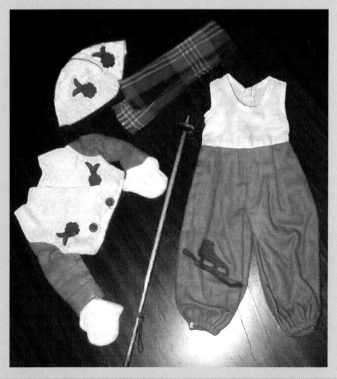

Skiing outfit for 14" DEBU'TEEN. Sold for $52.00, internet auction. Courtesy of Kandie Silveira.

In the Spring of 1937, new girl dolls began appearing in Arranbee's advertisements. First, there was a composition and cloth child that was more than a baby doll but not quite a full girl doll. An advertisement in the April issue of *Playthings* of that year states her name as Nannette Mama Doll. The cloth torso on this doll had 'swing' legs, meaning that the upper part of her legs was cloth, with stitching across the hip line. This construction made her look rather awkward standing, but was most appealing when seated. Her clothes were also quite different from the later girl dolls; they tended to be more childish, with a cotton pinafores and a matching undergarment with bloomer legs that could double as a playsuit. Nannette Mama Dolls have human hair or mohair wigs, and metal or glassene sleeping eyes. They may be marked R&B on either their heads or on the inside of their limbs. A curious note about this particular mama doll: although she began with the "Nanette" spelling, advertisements in *Playthings*, beginning in the summer of 1937, spelled her name with an extra *n* in the middle — "Nannette." The authors' collection of Arranbee advertisements from 1937 to 1943 carry this latter spelling until March of 1943, when the company reverted to its original spelling with one *n*. Boxes for this doll are found with the Nannette spelling. Note, too, that the spelling for the later hard plastic girl with the same name has only the one *n*.

18" NANNETTE. Marked R&B. Composition swivel head on shoulder plate, and composition limbs on stuffed cloth Mama type body. Wrist tag states her name as "Nannette — Walking and Talking Doll," although she was advertised as "Nannette Mama Doll." Original dress, with separate bolero jacket and matching romper. Human hair wig, brown glassene eyes, and open mouth. She is all original.
$332.00, internet auction.

Closeup of 18" NANNETTE showing original hair set and dress detail.

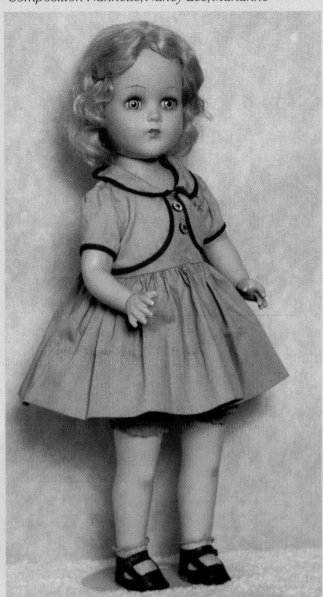

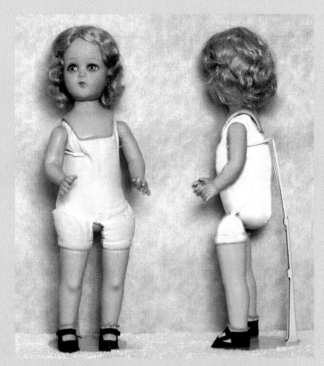

17" NANNETTE. View of body construction showing her swing legs, typical of the mama dolls.

17" NANNETTE. Marked R&B. Same doll as the previous one but having a different color combination on the clothes. All original with mohair wig and metal eyes.

23" NANNETTE. Swivel head on shoulder plate; cloth torso and swing legs. Open mouth and human hair wig. Scottie dog decoration on pinafore; coordinated romper and bonnet. Head is unmarked; R&B on upper arms. Original labeled box. $495.00.

Box for 23" NANNETTE.

Romper on 23" NANNETTE MAMA DOLL.

R&B mark on arm of 23" NANNETTE.

21" NANNETTE. Composition and cloth, all original.
Wrist tag shows the original spelling of her name.
Marilee Lindgren Collection.

A variation of the Nannette Mama Doll is Marianne. A larger composition and cloth child, she came in organdy dresses and bonnets, with a human hair wig; she was no doubt a more expensive doll. Although found unmarked, the label on her original dress states her name. As with other unmarked dolls, only the dress label can identify her.

In 1943, a true girl doll of all composition appeared: Nancy Lee was a pre-teen girl that today is sometimes confused with the Debu'teen doll. Nancy Lee, however, had a bit of a sweeter, more roundish face, as well as a younger appearance; Debu'teen, slimmer in both face and body, was meant to look like a teenager and was always promoted as such. Nancy Lee did, however, have as great a variety of dresses and gowns as the teenage doll. By the time that Arranbee advertisements promot-

ing Nancy Lee began appearing in March of 1943, the Debu'teen name was no longer present. Nancy Lees are usually marked R&B, but as with other dolls, she can be found with no markings at all.

It should be noted that a few of the Nancy Lee dolls found today are not of Arranbee's usual high quality. The finish on the composition, especially on the legs, can be rather rough. Also, the clothing is often missing the fine attention to detail found in the company's other doll clothes. The clothing styles, however, are very appealing. Apparently these dolls were manufactured expressly for a retail outlet or for a mail order catalog, as they mainly appear in plain shipping cartons without an Arranbee label.

24" MARIANNE. Unmarked shoulderhead. Human hair wig in original blond corkscrew curls, blue glassene eyes, and open mouth. Very detailed, original green organdy dress has a label stating her name. Matching bonnet. With leather shoes, she was obviously an expensive doll for her time. $375.00.

Closeup of MARIANNE.

Nancy Lee foil tag.

17" NANCY LEE. Marked R&B. Brown mohair wig, brown eyes. All original, in blue velvet dress and matching bonnet, cotton one-piece undergarment with lavender bows on bloomer legs, blue leatherette shoes. Tatted lace is sewn into the neckline and attached at the bodice with a blue button. $165.00.

17" NANCY LEE. Marked R&B. Blond mohair braids and blue eyes. Colorful cotton dress has organdy blouse effect. Oilcloth shoes with ties. All original in original shipping carton.

17" NANCY LEE. Marked R&B. All original, in pink sheer dress that has a gold flecked design. Mohair wigs like this one tend to be found matted in the back, either from lying in the box or from a bonnet.

18" NANCY LEE. Blond mohair wig, brown eyes. Original white and red organdy dress; hat, shoes, and socks not original. Sold for $150.00 in 1998.

14" NANCY LEE. All original, in red plaid taffeta dress and with hat and purse.
Carol J. Lindeman Collection.

15" NANCY LEE. Composition marked R&B. Blond mohair wig, blue tin eyes. Original magenta jumper dress has organdy sleeves; appropriate hat, shoes, and socks. Sold for $195.00 in1999.

14" NANCY LEE. All composition, marked R&B. Original, dark peach silk dress has bands of blue and a separate fichu that crosses the bodice in front and buttons onto the back. This is a popular design found on the composition Arranbee dolls.

14" NANCY LEE. Original red flowered dress has separate fichu; doll has one-piece undergarment. Hat is questionable, shoes have been replaced.

14" Composition GIRL AND BOY. These are not twins, as the girl has brown eyes and the boy has blue, but they both have blond, human hair wigs (as state their wrist tags). Both are all original.
Anita Maxwell Collection.

Undergarment on girl, and back view of boy showing button on shorts.

14" NANCY LEE. Similar doll to the preceding, with some variations in dress and eye color.
Millie Caliri Collection.

**17" NANCY LEE. Full composition. Green coat and matching hat,
coordinated with a pink dress that has a green floral print. Oilcloth shoes.
Nancy Lee foil tag and original, dime store price tag.** *Anita Maxwell Collection.*

**20" NANCY LEE. Variation of preceding doll; red coat
is unlined, with matching hat and heavy
cotton plaid dress. Original outfit; shoes are reproduction of old ones. Brown eyes and dark blond wig.
Marked R&B. $175.00.**

14" NANCY LEE. Brown mohair wig and blue eyes. Coordinated outfit of yellow print dress under tan pile coat; brown felt hat. All original, in displayed only condition. 1998 price was $275.00.

18" Composition. Marked R&B. Mohair wig, light blue eyes. Suede type cloth dress has tatting and red trim. Arranbee features on dress indicate that it is almost certainly original. Diana Gibson Collection

18" Composition. Marked R&B with blue eyes. Plaid taffeta dress has white cotton sleeves, yoke, and collar, and a brown belt. Faux fur jacket is lined with dress material. Shoes and socks also original. Diana Gibson Collection.

18" SOUTHERN SERIES. Marked R&B. Composition Nancy Lee doll with human hair wig. Very detailed outfit with cutout design shoes. All original and obviously a very expensive doll when new. Anita Maxwell Collection.

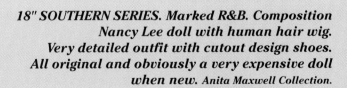

18" NANCY LEE. Marked R&B. Brown mohair wig and exceptionally light blue eyes. Original gown has lavender floral print and is made of a very silky material. Full slip, panties, shoes, and socks also original. Wig is an appropriate replacement. Coordinated color bow in her hair. $145.00.

18" SOUTHERN GIRL. *Composition girl with brown wig and eyes. All original variation of preceding doll.* Lynn Chambers Collection.

14" SOUTHERN GIRL. *Marked R&B. Blond mohair wig. Blue on white background gown has bound scalloped edging on hem.* Anita Maxwell Collection.

18" SOUTHERN SERIES. *Marked R&B, often referred to as "Scarlett." Dark brown wig and eyes. All original, with hat variation and hem lace trimmed instead of bound.* Lynn Chambers Collection.

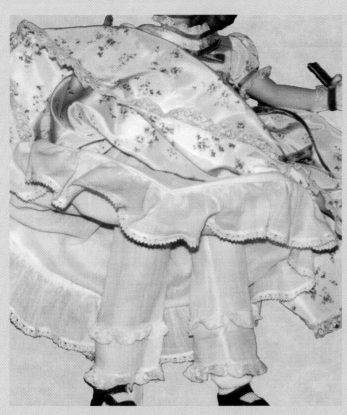

Typical undergarments found on Southern Series girls, as well as on other Arranbee composition girls.
Anita Maxwell Collection.

18" SOUTHERN GIRL. Human hair wig on this one. Gown variation has green accents and a lace edged hem.
Anita Maxwell Collection.

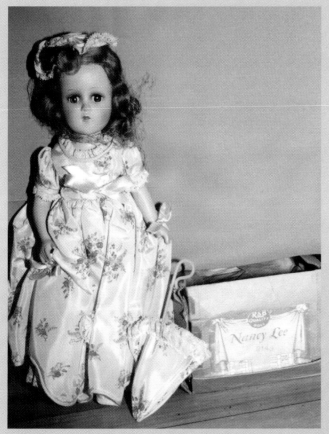

18" NANCY LEE. Larger floral print on this gown, with matching parasol. All original, with box. Several sources have attributed the clothes design to the noted designer Schiaparelli.
Kathleen Tornikoski Collection, photo by Judith Izen.

14" SOUTHERN GIRL. Marked R&B. Another variation of preceding gowns — this one has pink accents. Anita Maxwell Collection.

21" NANCY LEE. Mohair wig and brown eyes. All original. Lynn Chambers Collection.

14" NANCY LEE. Yellow formal has rosebud print and matching bow of dress material; yellow oilcloth shoes. All original.

13" Composition. Marked R&B with mohair wig and brown eyes. Flocked organza over taffeta under dress, with organza scarf and wristlets; coordinated evening purse and pin at bodice.
Diana Gibson Collection.

17" NANCY LEE. Marked R&B. Tosca mohair wig and brown eyes. Crimson velvet bows and hair feather accent formal gown of ivory tulle over taffeta. Cape is made of real fur and is lined. Fancy, red snap shoes. $295.00.

14" NANCY LEE. Marked R&B. Blue eyes, light brown mohair wig. All original, pink organza gown studded with silver dots, real fur jacket, pink leatherette shoes with cutout design.

Face of 14" NANCY LEE. Note her hat detail and bright blue eyes.

Gown detail of 14" NANCY LEE.

14" NANCY LEE. Marked R&B. Bright blue eyes, human hair blond wig. All original, in pink gown and panties, fabulous fur jacket, and pink shoes with cutout design.

21" NANCY LEE. Composition, with vivid blue eyes. All original pink flocked gown and fur cape.

Detail of gown on 21" NANCY LEE.

18" NANCY LEE. All composition, with blond mohair wig. All original, in flocked blue gown and matching cap. $325.00.

Pair of NANCY LEEs. All original — gowns are fragile. Sold for $500.00 in 1998.

17" NANCY LEE. Marked R&B, all original, with wrist tag. Mint doll has a human hair wig in its original set, detailed accessories (which are so often missing) on outfit, and green shoes with cutout design. $600.00.

17" NANCY LEE. Back view.

14" NANCY LEE. *Very tan appearance; marked R&B. Hat and shoes appear original; dress is finely hand-made cotton.*

14" NANCY LEE. *Marked R&B. Blond mohair wig and light blue eyes. Sunsuit and roller skates are extras found in a Nancy Lee trunk.*

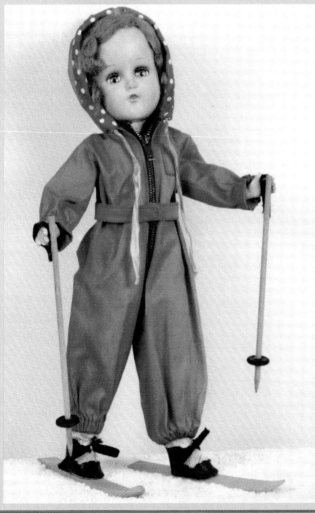

14" SKIER. *Marked R&B, all composition. Light blue eyes, closed mouth, brown mohair wig. Original red ski suit (also available in light green and tan). Old skis and poles. $195.00.*

18" SKATER. Composition, marked R&B. All original brown and tan skating outfit with skating pair silhouette. Mittens and skate blades are missing. $285.00.

14" NANCY LEE SKATER. Marked R&B. Fleece and velvet skating outfit, with original foil tag and red show ribbon.
Anita Maxwell Collection.

14" SKATER. Marked R&B, she wears her original skating dress and bonnet. This is a most unusual girl doll, as she has painted eyes. Sold on internet auction for $93.89. Better photograph not available.
Collection of Sue Wnek.

20" NANCY LEE. All original, in peach skating outfit and marked R&B on her head. Sold for $352.00 on internet auction.
Joan DiFiore Collection.

Appearing in the early 1940's was a pair of very unique composition dolls using the Nancy Lee model. Marked R&B, the 18" girl and boy appeared with blond human hair wigs and very colorful Norwegian outfits. The design and execution of the clothes on this pair is exceptional, even for Arranbee. The person to whom the authors sold this pair was of Norwegian descent, and verified that the dolls were indeed dressed authentically for one of the regions of Norway.

17" NORWEGIAN PAIR. Composition, marked R&B, modeled after Nancy Lee. Very detailed, authentic outfits are made of wool and leather. The boy is holding the Norwegian flag. An exceptional and rare pair of dolls. $500.00 for the pair in 1995; they are easily worth double that today.

Closeup of NORWEGIAN PAIR.

Other international dolls included Swiss, Dutch, and Scottish, and a special 16" doll named Miss International who came boxed with four different outfits: Swiss, Dutch, American, and Mexican. She was full composition and marked Design/Pat. Pend. on her head

One of several composition Arranbee girl dolls in the 1930's was Gloria Jean. This doll was based on the child movie star of that name; she was noted as having vivid blue eyes and a fuller face than the Nancy Lee doll. The child actress starred in the 1940 movie *A Little Bit of Heaven*, as a 12-year-old singer supporting her family. Another girl seen in various doll books is Nancy Jean. Unfortunately, we were unable to find examples of either of these dolls to photograph. However, two other variations of the Nancy Lee face are shown in the following photographs:

15" SCOTTISH GIRL. Marked R&B. Attention to detail and typical Scottish girl appearance. Appears to have been specifically dressed for a special event.

20" CAROLYN the SNOW QUEEN. Composition 1942. Blond mohair wig, blue eyes. This exact doll is shown in Pat Smith's Modern Collectors Dolls, Fourth Series, with a note from the author attached to her dress. Faint R&B on head. 1997 price was $225.00.

Prices for Nannette, Nancy Lee, Marianne, and other composition girl dolls:

Mint doll in original formal outfit, with box and tag. $800.00+.

Mint doll in day wear or sporting outfits, with box and tag: $500.00+.

Excellent condition with original clothes, displayed only, with light craze: $185.00 – 500.00 (depending on rarity of costume).

Played with condition with original clothes: $95.00 – 145.00.

Dirty, crazed, not original: $35.00 – 75.00.

17" R&B NUN. All composition, all original. 1997 price was $250.00.
Jeanne Melanson Collection.

At the New York Toy Fair in the Spring of 1947, Arranbee introduced its "new and improved" line of dolls. The Company's announcement in *Playthings*, February 1947, noted that the "colorful costumes are, as usual, keynoted by modern designs and advanced styling that customers naturally expect in an Arranbee creation. We are confident that you will agree that our 1947 line adds new laurels to our reputation as producers of quality dolls at popular prices."

The introduction of plastic brought new possibilities to the manufacture of dolls. The hard plastic girl dolls were more durable than previous ones of composition, and reflected the growing role of women outside the home through the variety of their costumes. The two prominent Arranbee girl dolls of this era were Nanette and Nancy Lee. Distinguishing between these two is difficult without the presence of a wrist tag or original box label. Nanette and Nancy Lee made with the painted hard plastic of the first dolls, however, did have a small but noticeable difference: Nanette tended to have a more pointed chin with a narrower face, while Nancy Lee had a rounder, wider face. With the development of flesh-colored plastic, this difference become markedly absent. To complicate the matter further, Arranbee sometimes advertised a doll as Nanette, then sold her in a box with a Nancy Lee label. The hard plastic Nanette doll should not be confused with the composition and cloth Nannette Mama doll as they are two entirely different dolls. Nanette and Nancy Lee dolls were produced for about a decade.

The variety of clothing appearing on these girl dolls was outstanding, with outfits ranging from day dresses to gowns, as well as such specialty clothing as cowgirl and majorette outfits. All of the ensembles came with many accessories. These accessories included hats, bonnets, wristlets, shoulder bags, purses, mittens and scarfs, etc., all coordinated to the individual outfit. The fur jackets accompanying the evening gowns were made of rabbit fur. Tied to the wrists of many of the dolls were colorful ribbons, often missing today. Shoes were sometimes color matched to the particular outfit, white shoes being seen mainly with daytime dresses. Storybook outfits were also produced, and included Cinderella and Alice in Wonderland. Many of the hard plastic girls also came in trunks or suitcases with extra outfits, and most carried pink flexible curlers on their wrist tags.

Arranbee used several different materials for their wigs on these hard plastic girls. Floss wigs were done quite elaborately on the ballerinas and dolls in long gowns; these wigs could not be easily restyled, as combing broke the floss strands. Mohair wigs were also used, but though mohair is more durable than the floss, it is still quite fragile for restyling as it tends to mat and frizz. Occasionally, a human hair wig may be found, but these were on the more expensive dolls. Later wigs gave way to the new materials Dynel and Saran. Dynel is soft and easily curled, and many of the hard plastic girl dolls appear with flexible plastic curlers attached to their wrist tags. Saran varies in softness, and the nylon wigs, while more durable, have more rigid fibers than any of the previous materials and are not easily curled; Saran is generally used in braids. Many of the nylon wigs have a very shiny appearance and are not natural looking.

Note that the dolls in this chapter are not arranged by date of manufacture, but are instead loosely grouped by outfits for comparison.

By 1952, Nanettes were also available as walking dolls, some with knee joints. There were two walker bodies: a modified hard plastic body and a pin-jointed one. Both of these were also available with vinyl heads. The face of the vinyl-headed version of Nanette is squarer, and the appearance is quite different from the hard plastic heads; they can be found starting on page 186.

In early 1952, Nanette received a very unique promotion, as reported in the March issue for that year by *Playthings*: Vera Ellen, the MGM dancing actress, was photographed with a Nanette doll. Miss Ellen, the article noted, said that Nanette "was the doll she loved best." As part of a personal tour, which was made in conjunction with the opening of the technicolor musical *Belle of New York*, in which Fred Astaire co-starred with the actress, she presented Nanette dolls to hundreds of crippled children. In February, when she arrived in her home town of Cincinnati, she was honored with a birthday party to which a group of some 400 children had been invited. Instead of receiving gifts herself, the actress gave over 50 Nanette dolls to those children who had birthdays in the same month.

14" Nancy Jane was advertised for only a short period of time during 1954, and is a doll seldom seen today. Since she resembles other dolls which are also marked Made in USA, she is difficult to identify unless she has the addition of R&B on her head, or any identifying tags. Nancy Jane came in a suitcase with a wardrobe and many accessories; her clothes were actually the same as Nanette's. The trunk sticker reads, "An Arranbee Doll," and her wrist tag bears her name. A Nancy Lane doll listed in an article in *Playthings* may actually be just a typographical error, as no other reference to this name was found.

For other Arranbee dolls of this period see Appendix II: Arranbee Dolls Found in Other Doll Books.

Prices for Nanette and Nancy Lee dolls:
Mint doll in original formal outfit, with box and tag: $900.00+.
Mint doll in day wear or sporting outfits, with box and tag: $450.00+.
Excellent condition with original clothes, displayed only: $195.00 – 500.00 (depending on rarity of costume).
Played with condition with original clothes: $95.00 – 145.00.
Dirty, not original: $35.00 – 85.00.

17" NANETTE. Strung girl marked R&B. Original, pink organdy dress with lace details and fabric flowers on the skirt, black oilcloth snap-front shoes. Hair ribbons have been replaced on mohair wig. Excellent condition. $325.00 in 2000.

Ad for NANETTE in September 1950 Playthings.

20" NANCY LEE. Mint in original box. Childhood doll of Ann Tardy.

20" NANETTE. Blond wig is made of mohair. Pale pink dress has tiny accordion pleated skirt and neck ruffle, accented with blue ribbons and pink flowers at the waist; snap-front shoes. She is all original, displayed only condition.
Sherri van Opijnen Collection.

14" NANETTE. Strung hard plastic, with R&B mark on head. Strawberry blond saran wig, medium blue eyes. Embroidered fichu buttons across front of pale pink nylon dress. Pink oilcloth shoes. As with some other Arranbee hats, this one appears too small, but it is original. Doll has uneven coloring on arms and legs. $235.00.

14" NANETTE BALLERINA. All original, in pink satin tutu with maribu trim; matching panties.
Mary Davis Collection.

14" NANETTE. Unmarked strung doll. Mohair braids, blue sleep eyes. White cotton dress has pastel blue dots; organdy pinafore. All original. $225.00.

14" NANCY LEE BALLERINA. Strung girl is all original, in yellow and gold tutu, with wrist tag.
Anita Maxwell Collection.

14" NANETTE BALLERINA. Marked R&B. Same outfit as preceding doll, but in pink. Elaborate wig is made of floss and styled differently. Floss wigs like this are almost impossible to restyle. $325.00.

Head view of 14" Ballerina showing the different, elaborate floss wig.

14" NANETTE. Original blue cotton dress has offset pink bodice detail. Shoes are not original.
Mary Davis Collection.

14" NANCY LEE SQUARE DANCE. Hard plastic girl, marked R&B. Blond floss wig, blue eyes. Handkerchief is pinned at the waist of her cotton dress (to wipe the perspiration off her forehead after dancing!). Red oilcloth shoes. This outfit also came in blue with blue shoes. $450.00.

14" SCHOOL DAYS NANCY LEE . Strung doll, marked R&B. Mohair wig in original braids. Blue cotton dress has puff sleeves; separate organdy pinafore with ABC print. Blue oilcloth shoes; blue hat that has faded to purple. Her school slate is missing, but the rest is all here, and original. This outfit also came in red with red shoes. $251.00, 2000 internet auction.

14" NANCY LEE. Original dress has apron effect with strawberry trim; shoes not original.
Mary Davis Collection.

14" NANETTE. Hard plastic walker, marked R&B. Green dress is original; shoes are replaced. $165.00.

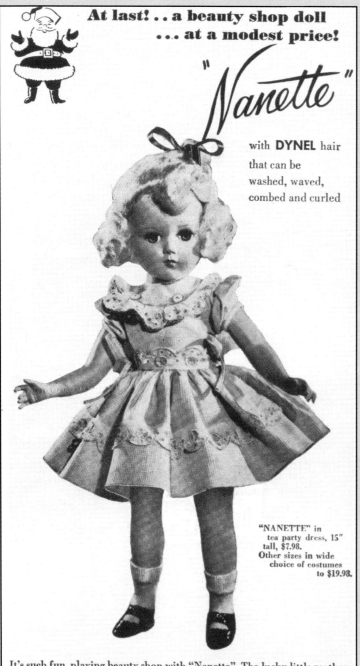

At last! .. a beauty shop doll
... at a modest price!

"Nanette"

with **DYNEL** hair
that can be
washed, waved,
combed and curled

"NANETTE" in
tea party dress, 15"
tall, $7.98.
Other sizes in wide
choice of costumes
to $19.98.

It's such fun, playing beauty shop with "Nanette". The lucky little mother who gets her can shampoo Nanette's hair again and again. She can curl it on Nanette's own curlers and set in *any* hair-do. Nanette *has a winsome* face with eyes that move appealingly. Her arms, legs, head and body are all plastic, won't crack, peel or chip—washable. And like all Arranbee dolls, she's made for years of active play. You'll find her and all the Arranbees at your favorite store; or write for the address nearest you.

Advertisement for NANETTE BEAUTY SHOP doll wearing tea party dress. From unknown magazine.

17" NANETTE in tea party dress. Pique dress is light yellow with blue banded sleeves. Cord bows accent the waist, with a large self bow in the back. Original snap-front shoes and under-clothes. Wig is made of Dynel.

20" NANCY LEE ROLLER SKATER. Mint in box sold for $500.00 at 2000 auction. *Courtesy of McMasters Doll Auctions.*

14" NANETTE. Golden blond strung girl, marked R&B, in original organdy dress. Blue metal trunk holds several original outfits. $395.00.

17" NANETTE. Marked R&B. Reddish brown wig and high color. Original brown organdy dress has basket design; hat and shoes are not original. $190.00.

18" NANETTE. All original; blue and white dress is variation of the preceding doll's. Wig is a replacement. *Robert Modena Collection.*

Puppy hat on 14" Nanette Roller Skater.

14" NANETTE ROLLER SKATER. *Original taffeta and organdy dress has "I Love You" decorative braid; original red shoe skates. Felt hat has puppy decoration — it is not known if this is original.*

Mary Davis Collection.

17" ALICE IN WONDERLAND. *Hard plastic walker. Golden blond wig and blue sleeping eyes. All original, in traditional Alice outfit. Excellent condition throughout. $325.00.*

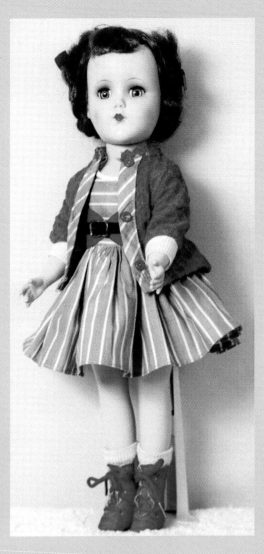

14" NANETTE. Strung doll, marked R&B. Red school-house motif on dress. All original. See this outfit in blue on Nancy Jane, later in this chapter.
Diana Gibson Collection.

14" NANETTE. Hard plastic walker, marked R&B on her head and Made in USA on her back. Brunette saran braids are looped at the sides. All original, but blades are missing from the skates. $195.00.

14" NANETTE. Strung doll marked R&B. Original red checked jumper-effect dress, with hat and oilcloth shoes.

18" NANETTE. Coordinated plaid skirt and jacket; straw hat and saddle shoes. Can also be seen with red and white saddle shoes. All original.
Anita Maxwell Collection.

18" NANETTE. Hard plastic, wearing a different color combination of the same outfit as the preceding doll. All original. Sold for $165.00 in 1998.

"Beauty Shop" Walking Doll
NANETTE

Imagine, when led by the hand, Nanette *walks*, turns her head from side to side . . . sits, too. Her Saran hair can be washed, waved, combed and curled; comes with her own curlers and simple hair-do instructions. She's all-plastic — won't crack, peel or chip — has moving eyes. Beautifully dressed, in party dress, petticoat, panties and shoes. 15" tall. $7.98.†
Other sizes up to $19.98.†

R & B DOLL COMPANY
200 Fifth Ave., New York 10, N. Y.

1952 NANETTE advertisement from unknown magazine showing party dress.

20" NANETTE. *Marked R&B. Organdy yellow and brown party dress, yellow socks, brown leatherette shoes are original; hair ribbons replaced. This dress also came in other colors, including blue. The preceding 1952 advertisement for this doll describes her as a walker, but this doll is strung. $250.00.*

14" NANETTE. *Original red and white dress has attached apron and coordinates with a Littlest Angel dress.*
Millie Caliri Collection.

14" NANETTE. *Strung doll, marked R&B. The dress she wears is white cotton, with a separate pinafore. Red leatherette shoes snap in the center. Brunette wig in original braids. All original doll has extra, original clothes in her trunk.*
Diana Gibson Collection.

NANETTE ROLLER SKATER — With lovely genuine SARAN wig, wide-belted plaid jumper skirt, cute peasant blouse, big matching hair ribbon. Wearing roller skates and carrying extra shoes. 15", 18", 23" — to retail from $7.98.

NANETTE DOLLS ARE OF UNBREAKABLE PLASTIC
ALL NANETTE WIGS CAN BE WASHED, SHAMPOOED, COMBED AND SET — COMB, CURLERS AND 2-COLOR INSTRUCTION SHEET PROVIDED WITH EACH DOLL.

Advertisement in **Playthings** *for Nanette Roller Skater.*

14" NANETTE. Hard plastic walker. Plastic belt has Cracker Jack type boot and flat iron charms. Hair has been trimmed in back and hat is a replacement; the rest is all original. Original box has her name. This outfit also came in a blue version.

14" NANETTE ROLLER SKATER. All original. $756.00, 2000 internet auction.
From the Frances DePaoli Collection; photograph by Mike Fornier.

14" NANETTE. Special attention to Arranbee details makes this girl appear completely original, but she is an exceptionally fine example of re-dressing.
Robert Modena Collection.

Pair of 17" and 14" NANETTES, wearing variations of the same dress. All original.
Anita Maxwell Collection.

14" NANETTE WALKER. Marked R&B. Original blue taffeta dress, underclothes, shoes, and socks; black belt and hat are missing.

18" NANETTE WALKER. Same dress as on preced-ing doll, with color variation. Original, but miss-ing black belt and black shoes.
Carol J. Lindeman Collection.

17" NANETTE ROLLER SKATER. Hard plastic walker with red braids. Original red plaid dress; red bloomer panties. Red roller skates and hat are replacements.

Give her the "beauty shop" doll that walks..*Nanette*"

with Saran hair...thriftily priced at $7.98 to $19.98
(slightly higher on West Coast)

Nanette's an all-round play girl. Sits up smart as anything. Has Saran hair that can be washed, waved, combed and curled. Lead her by the hand and she'll step right out, moving her head as she goes. Nanette's entirely washable, durable plastic from head to toe—won't crack, chip or peel—ready for years of play. Comes in 14 different styles, each in three sizes: 15", 18", 23". Look for her and all the other lovable R & B dolls at your favorite store; or write for the address nearest you.

Advertisement for the BEAUTY SHOP DOLL, a walker that wears a scalloped taffeta dress.

17" NANETTE. Right out of the preceding advertisement. Wig is from another Arranbee doll and shoes are not original. $85.00.

Back view of 20" NURSE, showing the unique styling of her original mohair braids.

20" NURSE. Nancy Lee face on this strung girl, marked R&B. She appears to be all original, but this has not been verified.

18" NANETTE WALKER. Fashionable suit with shoulder bag and hat. This outfit is number #7115. Mint doll. Carole J. Lindeman Collection.

17" NANETTE. Brunette walker is unplayed with; original red dress has fruit trim. This is a very distinctive design and has been referred to as "Calypso," but this name has not been verified.

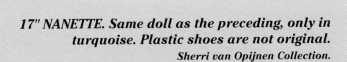

17" NANETTE. Original blue checked suit is a variation of the preceding doll's.
Millie Caliri Collection.

17" NANETTE. Same doll as the preceding, only in turquoise. Plastic shoes are not original.
Sherri van Opijnen Collection.

14" NANCY LEE. Saran wig on strung doll. Blue satin gown shows typical Arranbee binding detail. **Anita Maxwell Collection.**

14" NANETTE. Strung, with saran wig. Floral taffeta gown has satin collar and coordinated bows decorating the skirt. **Anita Maxwell Collection.**

18" PINK PROM. All original, ruffled pink gown. Bouquet has been added. **Hally Smith Collection.**

21" NANCY LEE. Strung doll, marked R&B. Dark brown wig. All original slate blue gown with big bows and pink flowers. Displayed only doll. $595.00

17" NANETTE WALKER. Original flocked formal gown. Evening bag has been added. Tiara is missing. This is either Princess Juliana or "Queen of the Ball," depending on promotion.
Millie Caliri Collection.

Advertisement in Playthings *for*
NANETTE PARTY FORMAL.

17" NANETTE PARTY FORMAL. All original, in pink chiffon gown and picture hat, with pink shoes. Skirt has repairs, otherwise a displayed only doll.

14" BRIDESMAID. Pale blue organdy gown with pink trim and pink hat. Mohair wig. Mint in box doll with original price tag.
Anita Maxwell Collection.

17" NANETTE in EVENING GOWN. *Hard plastic walker, marked R&B. Brunette wig. Original gown; separate hoop skirt and evening bag. Snap-front satin evening shoes.*

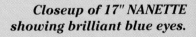

18" BRIDESMAID. *Mohair wig in original set. Ruffled pink gown in the reverse colors of the preceding gown. All original, mint doll.*
Lynn Chambers Collection.

Closeup of 17" NANETTE showing brilliant blue eyes.

17" BRIDE. Marked R&B, hard plastic with auburn wig. Ivory flocked bridal gown with train; separate slip also has train, matching panties; crown headpiece has double layer veil. All original doll.

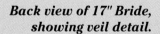

Back view of 17" Bride, showing veil detail.

Another variation of the bridal veil treatment with original outfit. $295.00.

17" NANCY LEE BRIDE. *Similar gown, but having different head piece. Mohair wig in original set; all original with wrist tag. Sold in early 2000 internet auction for $406.00.*

Chapel cap and veil on 17" BRIDE.

14" NANCY LEE BRIDE. *Original bridal gown and veil. Tulle varies on bridal bouquet, so it may not be original.* Diana Gibson Collection.

20" NANETTE. All original, in elaborate formal gown of yellow nylon and damask with separate evening cape. Arranbee's attention to detail is abundantly evident throughout. Sherri van Opijnen Collection.

BRIDE. All original, in flocked gown.
Ronda Andrews Collection.

Back view of yellow formal.

17" NANETTE. *Hard plastic walker in gorgeous formal. Sheer over-dress has flocked flowers and lavender satin sash. Brilliant blue eyes and high facial color.*

18" NANCY LEE. *Walker is all original and wearing same gown as preceding doll, but having a rose satin bow.* **Diana Gibson Collection.**

18" NANCY LEE. *Strung girl, in blue brocade formal with real fur trim, a very formal outfit.* **Anita Maxwell Collection.**

Closeup showing floss wig and perfect facial coloring on 17" NANETTE.

17" NANETTE. Strung, high fashion. Mint doll with elaborate wig. Real fur on muff; sheer tulle duster with "jeweled" pin closure over ivory brocade gown. (In a recent year, a doll similar to this one sold for $1,000+ at auction.) Annette Davino Collection.

14" NANETTE. Strung doll. Same formal gown as preceding doll, but a variation without the duster.
Sherri van Opijnen Collection.

*Back view of elaborate hairdo on 14"
NANETTE.*

*NANETTE FLORAL FORMAL. Same as preceding doll,
showing detail of back of gown. All original.*
Sherri van Opijnen Collection.

*18" GIMBEL'S PARASOL FORMAL. Taffeta gown and
parasol, with Gimbel's department store tag.*
Hally Smith Collection.

Detail of gown underskirt on 17" NANETTE WALKER.

17" NANETTE WALKER. Marked R&B. Tulle over taffeta gown is Style #1566. All original, with saran wig.

14" NANETTE WALKER. Same gown as preceding doll, but this one is pink. All original.
Robert Modena Collection.

17" NANCY LEE. Floss hair. All original, plaid taffeta gown (matching purse missing). Designer styling on gown features a diagonal cut bodice with a bow tied on the left shoulder. Mary Davis Collection.

17" NANETTE WALKER. Taffeta and organdy dress with peasant style ruffled sleeves. All original. Marked R & B on head, Made in USA on back.

Head view of 17" Nanette Walker. Note the more pronounced turned-up nose.

14" NANETTE WALKER. Coordinated outfit in rose and blue (dress has probably faded, not uncommon in taffeta). Saran wig on an all original doll.
Anita Maxwell Collection.

14" GOLD SKATER. Skirt is a flannel type material; blouse is knitted with gold threads running through weave. All original, with hat and scarf (which are often missing). Anita Maxwell Collection.

14" NANETTE SKATER. Marked Made in USA on her back, R&B on her head. Three-piece skating outfit with poodle design. Original, but missing matching cap and scarf. Sold for $185.00 in 1999.

14" NANETTE SKATER. Strung hard plastic girl. Faint R&B. Original skating outfit of flannel type skirt attached to camisole top, with a separate fleece jacket that has a zipper closure. Original, but tam is missing. Brown mohair wig.

14" BLUE SKATER. Strung Nancy Lee doll marked R&B, 1949. All original, in blue felt skating outfit trimmed in white felt, with matching hat; white skates. Her brunette wig is made of mohair.
Anita Maxwell Collection.

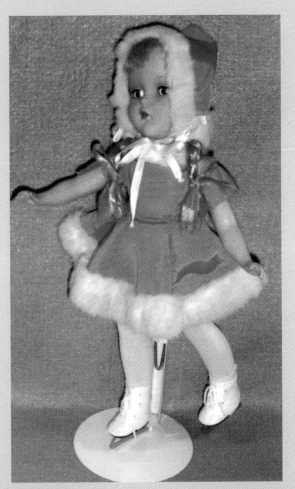

15" PINK SKATER. Original pink skating outfit with hood. Stockings and skates are not original.
Hally Smith Collection.

"SS R&B Contest" button on 17" Skater. No reference to actual contest has been found. This may have been a local event. Anita Maxwell Collection.

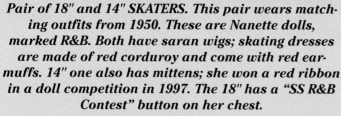

Pair of 18" and 14" SKATERS. This pair wears matching outfits from 1950. These are Nanette dolls, marked R&B. Both have saran wigs; skating dresses are made of red corduroy and come with red earmuffs. 14" one also has mittens; she won a red ribbon in a doll competition in 1997. The 18" has a "SS R&B Contest" button on her chest.
Anita Maxwell Collection.

21" SKATER. Strung girl, wearing all original skating outfit with skating pair silhouette. This outfit came in other colors (which can be seen on the composition skaters in Chapter 7).
Sherri van Opijnen Collection.

14" NANCY JANE. Strung hard plastic girl, marked Made in USA. Schoolhouse motif on organdy pinafore. All original, with suitcase and extra clothes. Doll is in excellent condition; wear on case. $433.00, internet auction.

Slippers for 14" Nancy Jane coordinate with her pajamas.

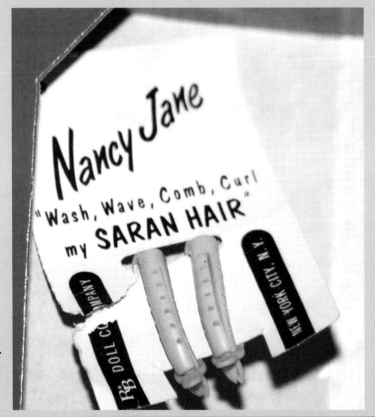

Closeup of 14" Nancy Jane tag with soft plastic curlers to set her saran hair.

14" and 18" NANCY LEES. Floss wigs on both dolls. These taffeta gowns are probably seen more often than other styles, but they are not always seen in this exceptional condition. Plaids will also be seen cut in different directions. Anita Maxwell Collection.

14" NANCY LEE. All original, in rose velvet gown with rabbit fur decoration and purse (usually missing). Blond floss wig in original set.
Anita Maxwell Collection.

14" NANCY LEE. Original rose velvet gown and matching hair decoration.

14" QUEEN of the BALL. Advertised in Orman's 1953 fall catalog. Ornate crown with rhinestones, on platinum blond wig. Strapless taffeta gown has tulle overlay, with an embroidered panel down the front, pearl shoulder accents, and flower spray at waist. R&B mark. $837.00, internet auction. Veronica Jochens Collection.

14" PRINCESS ELIZABETH with Baby Prince. Hard plastic strung doll, marked R&B. Light brown mohair wig has silver crown attached. Flocked pink chiffon gown, full length pink cotton slip with matching panties, and pink oilcloth shoes are all original. Baby is German bisque and is a replacement; the baby gown should be of the same material. Thought to commemorate the birth of Prince Charles in November of 1948, while Elizabeth was the heir to the throne.

Closeup of BRIDE, showing flocked heart detail on gown. This same material can be found on other Arranbee doll gowns (such as Littlest Angel Bride).

14" NANETTE BRIDE. Walking doll has jointed knees so she can sit. Layered gown has lace details and pearl necklace. Saran wig in original set.
Joan Willard Collection.

14" NANETTE WALKER. This doll is a 1952 variation of the walking doll, having pin-jointed hips and jointed knees. She also appeared with a vinyl head.

17" PRINCESS JULIANA. Hard plastic, all original. A royal appearance, with blue sash and crown. Believed to represent Princess Juliana of the Netherlands on the eve of her coronation in 1948.
Marilee Lindgren Collection.

23" SENORITA. Original and stunning black lace gown with very full veil in traditional styling. Vintage shoes not original.
Hally Smith Collection.

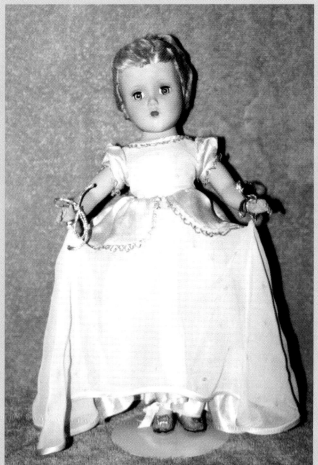

17" CINDERELLA. All original, in a traditional design of the gown, which has silver flecks throughout. She has "glass" slippers, also. Tag for this doll would have "Cinderella" on it. *Marilee Lindgren Collection.*

18" NANCY LEE. All original. This dress with its attached apron can also be found in red. *Susan Mason Collection.*

22" NANETTE peasant style dress made to appear as separate pieces. $38.99, internet auction.

A popular Arranbee doll of the years following WWII was Little Angel, a very appealing baby doll. Introduced in 1947, this latest Little Angel had a hard plastic head on a cloth body, and stuffed latex limbs that made the doll feel more like a real baby than the dolls with hard bodies felt. Unfortunately, the latex was prone to darkening, and exposure to heat would cause the material to either dry out and crack or to melt. When the limbs were changed to vinyl, the doll retained its original color much better and was more durable, but the vinyl easily picked up the soil from a child's hands. The shoulder area of the arms and the upper part of the legs were part of the cloth body. Dolls with full length latex or vinyl limbs were also produced, as well as all-vinyl bodies with flexible hips. The hard plastic heads came in both molded hair and wigged versions, and with open or closed mouths.

The Little Angel doll was used for "Rock Me Baby," a special doll with rock-to-sleep eyes that was introduced in June of 1954. Produced in 17" and 20" sizes, she was available with either latex or vinyl limbs. The eyes were unique on this doll; she would not close her eyes unless rocked to sleep either in the child's arms or in her cradle. Having originally applied in December of 1954, Arranbee obtained US Patent # 2,813,372 for this special feature on November 19, 1957. An article in the October 1954 issue of *Playthings* stated that Little Angel and Rock Me Baby were to be featured on Steve Allen's *Tonight* show, a popular program of the era. There were two different cradles for this doll. One was actually the doll's box with fold-out rockers; the other cradle was more substantial, being made of wood and wicker. Both cradles included a blanket and a pillow. The wicker cradle was obviously the more expensive model, and it had an attached music box.

Dream Baby, so popular as a bisque or composition head doll now, was made of all hard plastic and available either in standing or sitting models. The heads on these dolls only remotely resembled the earlier versions, but were just as cute, and these models had more definition and brighter facial coloring. The clothes on Dream Baby were also created with more detail.

By 1951, other babies appeared in the Arranbee line. These included Angel Face, Angel Skin, and Baby Bunting. The year 1951 also saw the first Arranbee doll ads appearing in national consumer magazines such as *Life,* and marked the beginning of the phrase "the dolls that sell on sight." Arranbee used this phrase throughout their advertisements in the 1950s.

Dolls not photographed:
18" Toddler. 1950s hard plastic head, cloth body, vinyl limbs. "250" on head.
10" Peachy. 1950's black hard plastic baby with painted side-glancing eyes and molded hole for ribbon; bent limbs. Unmarked.
Baby Bunting Twins. Markings unknown.

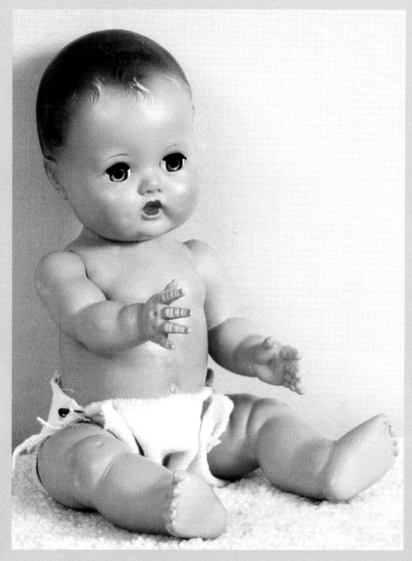

10" DREAM BABY. All original, in toddler boy's suit. He has his original paper tag, his store tag, and a Blue Ribbon from a show. His cap is missing.. This outfit also came in pink.
Anita Maxwell Collection.

10½" DREAM BABY.
This is the bent leg version; marked Arranbee.

10" DREAM BABY TWINS. Marked Arranbee on their heads. Vintage Arranbee clothes. $250.00.

Closeup of 15" LITTLE ANGEL.

15" LITTLE ANGEL. Late 1940's. Hard plastic head marked Arranbee. Pink cloth torso with vinyl limbs. Pink nylon baby dress bears her name. Pink cotton slip and booties. All original and unplayed with. $282.00 at auction.

Detail of gown on LITTLE ANGEL. This design is repeated all over the dress.

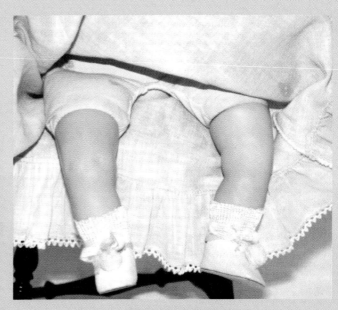

Detail of underclothes and body construction of LITTLE ANGEL.

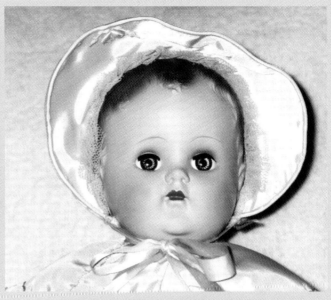

Closeup of 19" LITTLE ANGEL.
Cyndee Barlow Collection.

19" LITTLE ANGEL. Hard plastic; vinyl limbs on cloth
body. All original pink taffeta dress and bonnet.
Cyndee Barlow Collection.

22" LITTLE ANGEL. Caracul wig.
Original clothes. $250.00.

Closeup of 22" LITTLE ANGEL.

17" BABY DONNA. Hard plastic head marked R&B. Molded brown ringlets. Well sculptured vinyl limbs on cloth body. Vintage clothes. $100.00.

17" LITTLE ANGEL.
Suellen Musgrove Collection.

Magazine ad for ROCK ME BABY and other Arranbee dolls.

22" ROCK ME BABY. Hard plastic head; stuffed vinyl body. Eyes will only close when she is rocked to sleep. Original box converts to cradle. All original clothes. $145.00 to $250.00. She was also available in a pram suit.

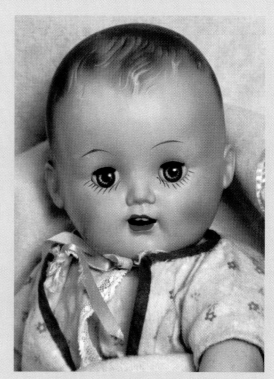

Closeup of ROCK ME BABY.

Cradle box is made of paperboard. Rockers fold flat under box.

LITTLE ANGEL. Original finish and coloring on her face make this doll exceptionally desirable.
Francesca Ellis Collection.

Little Angel Family
Little Angel, Littlest Angel,
Sweet Pea, Lil' Cupcake

Little Angel Family began in 1952 with the introduction of Little Angel, a 12" hard plastic toddler with straight legs and marked Pat. Pend. on her head. Arranbee bought Little Angel from another company, then dressed and marketed her. (Note that the Little Angel doll that Arranbee advertised in 1951 is a baby doll, not this toddler.) In 1953, Little Angel was noted as being "a sell-out at $3.98." Her little sister, Littlest Angel, was trademarked on June 29, 1954, and registered on May 31, 1956; she is marked R&B. With the arrival of her little sister, Little Angel was also available as a walker. By 1955, Littlest Angel was available with jointed knees and/or a vinyl head that had rooted hair. A 1958 advertisement shows her sporting her new Dutch Boy haircut. A variation in hair styling was the long-haired Littlest Angel, shown mint in her original box in this chapter; no advertisements were found for her and this is the only example the authors have. Another variation was the unusual hair coloring appearing during the mid-1950's: colors of red, green, and blue have been found.

Many of Littlest Angel's outfits were coordinated with her big sister's, as well as with those of the hard plastic Nanette doll, and some of the Coty Girl outfits resembled Littlest Angel clothing (the square dance dress, for one). An editorial found in *Playthings* in 1954 stated that merchants were complaining that they could not keep up with the demand for all the extra clothing available for these little dolls. This availability was a clever marketing strategy, and children clamored for these cute extra outfits that came in marked R&B boxes with cellophane windows. At the time of the 1955 Toy Fair, 36 separate outfits were available for Littlest Angel. Even pattern makers such as Butterick's began producing patterns specifically for making outfits for Littlest Angel. It appears that the smaller of the two dolls was more popular, perhaps due to the popularity of smaller dolls during this time period, and Little Angel no longer appeared in advertisements after the early part of 1955.

Accessories available separately for Littlest Angel included various travel bags, trunks, and display cases with a window for showing the doll. In addition, a 1954 Marshall Field & Co. catalog advertised Littlest Angel with a mahogany reproduction of a four-posted, early American Tester bed and a matching two-drawer wardrobe.

Prices for Little Angel Family dolls:
All original, mint in box: $150.00 – 450.00+.
Original clothes, no box: $75.00 – 150.00.
Nude, dirty, played with: $25.00 – 75.00.

Note that these price ranges are dependent on rarity, popularity, or outstanding presentation. Novelties such as Surprise Doll can vary from the above prices.

12" LITTLE ANGEL & 10" LITTLEST ANGEL wearing
matching checked overall outfits.
Marilyn McDonald Collection.

12" LITTLE ANGEL. Original flocked formal.
Marilyn McDonald Collection.

**12" LITTLE ANGELS. Checked overalls match
Littlest Angel's #028, 1954. Bridal gown match-
es Littlest Angel's #030 from 1955 brochure.
Hat replaces her veil.**
Marilyn McDonald Collection.

LITTLE ANGEL BRIDE. Original except for flowers.
Marilyn McDonald Collection.

LITTLE ANGEL TRIO. All are original.
Marilyn McDonald Collection.

Pair of LITTLE ANGELS. Lounging pajamas (?) and sunsuit from 1954.
Marilyn McDonald Collection.

12" LITTLE ANGEL. Original sunsuit, 1954. Matches Littlest Angel's 1954 Gay Sunsuit, #023.
Marilyn McDonald Collection.

2

Now! With Jointed Knees! 11" Tall!

Littlest Angel

is a real living doll! Goes everywhere, does everything!

Kneels, sits, walks, stands—washable Saran hair. 36 beautiful outfits.

Anything "mommy" can do "Littlest Angel" can do, too. With her jointed knees, she's 11" of lovable fun. She can be sponged, because she's all washable unbreakable plastic. Her lustrous, long Saran hair can be combed, washed, and set. She can be as well dressed as "mommy" for all her 36 outfits are carefully made, just like a real little girl's fashions. Give "Littlest Angel" to your own special little angel for any occasion — or make your gift of "Littlest Angel" an occasion in itself! Then add to "Littlest Angel's" wardrobe on birthdays, for Christmas, and all year 'round.

1010 — in panties, shoes and socks $2.98
36 beautiful outfits ....from 98c

1955 LITTLEST ANGEL brochure.

LITTLEST ANGEL. Outfit #026 from 1954. Same styling as the dress for the hard plastic Nanette.
Marilyn McDonald Collection.

SCHOOL DRESS. Same dress as preceding outfit, but different color.
Marilyn McDonald Collection.

Tennis Ensemble $1.49

Tennis, anyone? Today I wore my new tennis outfit. White shorts, and blue and white halter and shirt, with the cutest little tennis cap. I also have my own racket.

TENNIS ENSEMBLE, #041, from 1954 flyer.

Skating Costume $1.98

Down at the skating rink, I wear my pretty black felt costume with silver trimming and black hat to keep my hair in place. Notice my silver skates that glide me right along.

ICE SKATING, #053, 1954. Same as the advertisement in Playthings.

Picnic Outfit
055 . . . $1.98

I romp (now I've jointed knees) all over the picnic grounds, and everywhere people admire my dramatic black and white corduroy creation, with its rolled collar and stunning stripe effect. Sun glasses, too.

PICNIC, #055, 1954.

Roller Skating Set $2.49

Roller skating like I am here, or out hiking, my dungarees really can "take it", and they always look fine, 'specially when they have bright red polka dot cuffs, with matching handkerchief, halter and bonnet.

ROLLER SKATER, #062, from 1954 flyer.

LITTLEST ANGEL FISHERMAN, #071, 1954.
Marilyn McDonald Collection.

LITTLEST ANGELS. PRINT PARTY DRESS, #020 from 1955 and AFTERNOON DRESS, #025 from 1955. The afternoon dress was also available for Little Angel.
Marilyn McDonald Collection.

SUNSUIT & HAT, #022, 1955. Doll in box, with wrist tag.
Marilyn McDonald Collection.

**3-Piece Pajama Set
024 . . . $1.49**
I love to be an overnight guest when I have my three-piece pajama set to wear. It's all lacy and silken, with two-piece pajamas and elegant matching robe and slippers.

PAJAMA SET, #024, 1955.

10" LITTLEST ANGEL. 1955. *Brunette wig in original set with daisies. Extra boxed dress and shoes. This dress, #026, is redesigned from previous year but has the same catalog number. The boxed set includes a 32 page booklet showing the dolls fashions and some other Arranbee dolls; the doll also has her wrist tag. $450.00.*

***LITTLEST ANGEL in CHECKED OVERALLS, #028 from 1955. Catalog shows her with a matching bonnet, not a straw hat.* Private Collection.**

***LITTLEST ANGEL. Vinyl head. Original and boxed, with extra outfit (Checked Overalls #028) and booklet. $300.00 in August 2000.* Courtesy of McMasters Dolls Auctions.**

BRIDAL GOWN, #030, 1955. Pattern on gown is flocked hearts.

Bridal Gown
030 . . . $2.49
For my wedding day, I'll wear a beautiful bridal gown, embroidered all over with tiny flowers. My veil is of illusion net and I carry a bouquet of white blossoms.

BRIDAL GOWN. Same outfit number, but this one has flocked flowers.
Marilyn McDonald Collection.

Golf Outfit
038 . . . $1.98
A sports-minded woman like me needs these bright practical culottes on the golf course. And walking 18 holes is fun, 'cause now I've got jointed knees. My very own golf clubs, too, please note.

GOLF OUTFIT, #038, from 1955 brochure.

PARTY DRESS, #042 from 1954 and 1955, and unidentified dress with print of children on it.
Marilyn McDonald Collection.

**Bermuda Shorts
044 . . . $1.49**
Rough and tumble games
don't bother me when I wear
my navy blue tom-boy shirt,
picturing states of the union,
and my red Bermuda shorts.
A red ribbon keeps my Saran
hair in place.

***BERMUDA SHORTS. This is outfit #044, as shown in
the 1955 catalog.***

***ANGEL COSTUME. This is outfit #043 shown in the
1955 brochure.***
Marilyn McDonald Collection.

**Rain Coat
046 . . . $1.49**
Stormy days aren't hard to
take at all. Fact is I almost
like them when I wear my
rugged red plastic rain coat,
with the belted waist. The
hood protects my just-combed
Saran curls.

RAINCOAT, #046, 1955.

LITTLEST ANGEL CLOWN, #050 from 1955.
Marilyn McDonald Collection.

Little Angel Family

LITTLEST ANGEL wearing PARTY DRESS #051 from 1955 brochure. This outfit is identical to #506 in 1957 brochure. *Marilyn McDonald Collection.*

ICE SKATER. Outfit #052, 1955.
Marilyn McDonald Collection.

**Nurse's Uniform
054 . . . $1.98**
It's a snap to run to my patient's side now that I have jointed knees. An official red-lined cloak covers my easy-to-launder white nylon uniform. Authentic nurse's cap, too!

NURSE. Outfit #054, 1955.

PICNIC OUTFIT, #055, 1955. Purse is not original.
Marilyn McDonald Collection.

ARTIST. Outfit #056, 1955.
Marilyn McDonald Collection.

LITTLEST ANGEL in SKIRT & SWEATER, #057 from 1955. Catalog caption says she's "right in step for jitterbugging" wearing this outfit.
Marilyn McDonald Collection.

Red Riding Hood 059 . . . $1.98

Guess you know I'm Red Riding Hood, and I'm on my way to Grandmother's in my organdy print dress, topped by a bright red hood. I'm carrying a basketful of flowers.

RED RIDING HOOD. Littlest Angel outfit #059 on doll and from 1955 brochure. Photo shows her dress without the cape. Snap-front shoes are original. *Marilyn McDonald Collection.*

**Formal Gown
061 . . . $2.49**
Graduation time and here I am
in my lovely formal and petite
golden slippers. How I love to
dance in this beautiful dress
and hear it rustle!

FORMAL GOWN, #061, from 1955 catalog.

ROLLER SKATER, #062, 1955.
Marilyn McDonald Collection.

*TRIO of BALLERINAS. Center doll is wearing
outfit #063 from 1955. The other two have
vinyl heads and later outfits.*
Marilyn McDonald Collection.

LITTLEST ANGEL BALLERINA. Outfit is #063, 1955.
Marilyn McDonald Collection.

LITTLEST ANGEL COWGIRL, #064, 1955. This same design can be seen on the hard plastic Nanette.
Marilyn McDonald Collection.

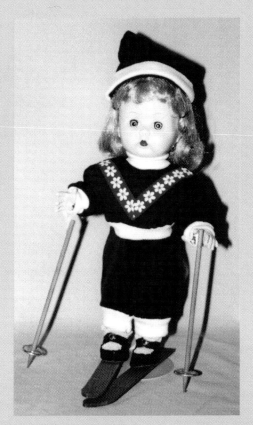

LITTLEST ANGEL SKIER, #065, 1955.
Diana Gibson Collection.

TV LOUNGING, #066, 1955. (#609 in 1957.) Note sunglasses — these were needed for glare from early TVs!
Marilyn McDonald Collection.

**Drum Majorette Costume
072 . . . $2.98**
Look at my high-stepping style now that I have jointed knees! I lead the parade in my drum majorette outfit — flare skirt, satin top, fancy boots, plumed hat, and whirling baton.

DRUM MAJORETTE, #072, 1955.

RIDING HABIT, #067, 1955. Cap and boots not original.
Private collection.

**Fur Coat Set
089 . . . $3.98**
A night "on the town" is what I'm anticipating as I don my most expensive furs...luxurious white fur. Matching fur hat and muff for elegance and warmth.

**Garment Bag
102 . . . $1.49**
As you can see, mommy and I are pretty fussy about my clothes. That's why this plaid garment bag is such a must for keeping my pretty things ready-to-wear.

LITTLEST ANGEL MAJORETTE. All original, but skirt has been cut off. $65.00.

FUR COAT SET, #089, 1955.

GARMENT BAG, #102, 1955.

**Travel Set
103 . . . $1.98**
No better way to keep frocks unwrinkled on the road than this plaid car bag, equipped with zipper and handle. Matching tote bag holds the things you need close at hand.

*TRAVEL SET, #103,
1955.*

**Travel Trunk
104 . . . $3.98**
Traveling is no easy task, you know, except when you use this metal travel trunk. Everything fits so nicely — never any wrinkles. A pull-out drawer for tiny articles. So easy to carry, too.

TRAVEL TRUNK, #104, 1955.

**Gretel Metal Trunk Set
151 . . . $9.98**
I've decked myself out as "Gretel", but this easy-to-carry sturdy metal trunk comes equipped with three others of my favorite outfits, complete right down to sun glasses, extra shoes and socks, and hangers.

GRETEL METAL TRUNK SET, #151, 1955.

**Riding Habit Metal Trunk
152 . . . $12.98**
Dressed for a weekend of horseback riding. Three other costumes, safe on hangers, are ready to go along, too, in this sturdy metal trunk. Sun glasses, extra shoes and socks, as well.

*RIDING HABIT METAL TRUNK SET,
#152, 1955.*

LITTLEST ANGEL in her plastic travel case. Right side holds her clothes. This case also came in red.
Marilyn McDonald Collection.

The Surprise Doll

In March of 1956, Arranbee advertised its "fabulous New Surprise Doll." Taken from the 1949 book *The Surprise Doll*, by Morrell Gipson, this Littlest Angel was a special promotion with six additional outfits, available separately, which depicted the outfits on the dolls shown in the book. These outfits were: Dutch, French, Chinese, Italian, Russian, and English. The doll came in a presentation box with graphics to make it look like a book itself; a pocket on the inside of the front cover held the little Wonder Book.

THE SURPRISE DOLL. 1957. Box has book appearance and shape. Holds doll and the original book by Wonder Books.

Back cover of box; it shows all the outfits.

Inside view of SURPRISE DOLL box, showing book and doll.

SURPRISE DOLL book. Tells the story of a little girl named Mary and her dolls.

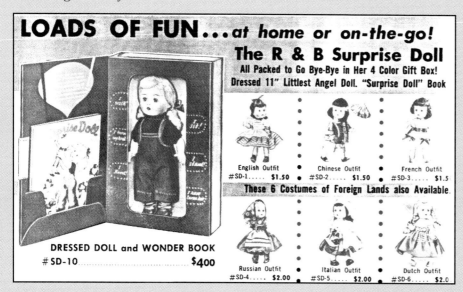

LOADS OF FUN...*at home or on-the-go!*
The R & B Surprise Doll
All Packed to Go Bye-Bye in Her 4 Color Gift Box!
Dressed 11" Littlest Angel Doll. "Surprise Doll" Book

English Outfit	Chinese Outfit	French Outfit
#SD-1..... $1.50	#SD-2..... $1.50	#SD-3..... $1.5

These 6 Costumes of Foreign Lands also Available.

Russian Outfit	Italian Outfit	Dutch Outfit
#SD-4..... $2.00	#SD-5..... $2.00	#SD-6..... $2.0

DRESSED DOLL and WONDER BOOK
#SD-10 .... **$4.00**

1955 brochure for SURPRISE DOLL showing her days-of-the-week outfits. The dolls wearing the different dresses are only drawings, not actual dolls.

SURPRISE DOLL. This is actually a special Littlest Angel, with orange hair and brown eyes.

SURPRISE DOLLS. Left to right: English, unknown, Russian, Italian, Dutch, Chinese. Surprise doll is in red overalls. Marilyn McDonald Collection.

FRENCH SURPRISE DOLL.
Marilyn McDonald Collection.

CHINESE SURPRISE DOLL. *Hallowe'en outfit on the right is a special design by Jude Ballantyne, creator of many unique outfits for Littlest Angel.*
Marilyn McDonald Collection.

her "Littlest Angel" changes moods with each new mode

Give "Littlest Angel" to your own special little angel. She's a full 11″ tall, kneels, sits, stands, moves her head as she walks. Her rooted blonde, brunette or honey color Saran hair can be washed, combed, curled. Wash her, she's sturdy plastic.
L83—"Littlest Angel" basic doll in panties, shoes, socks. Vinyl head, bob or pony style hairdo. 2.98
M83—Basic doll with hard head, braid or roll-back hairdo. 2.59
N83—Bride and trunk set. Basic doll plus bridal dress and full trousseau: sunsuit, short party dress, 3-piece pajama set, all accessories. In trousseau trunk. Set, 11.98
Following costumes sold separately:
P83—Bridal dress, embroidered net and taffeta, veil, bouquet, shoes. 2.49
Q83—Snug, cosy knitted 2-piece sleeper, duck applique. 1.00
R83—Pajama and Negligee ensemble, silky print, lace trim, slippers. 1.49
S83—Braid-trimmed party coat and hat plus Christmas dress, shoes, socks. 2.98
T83—Bouffant party dress, lace and ribbon trimmed, golden slippers. 1.49
U83—Gibson Girl blouse, pleated skirt, hat, shoes, bag, belt. .1.98

G. FOX & CO. TOYLAND, ELEVENTH FLOOR

1956 advertisement for LITTLEST ANGEL in G. Fox advertisement.
From the collection of Marge Meisinger; photograph by Suzanne Silverthorn.

***LITTLEST ANGELS** wearing original two-piece **KNIT SLEEPERS** in various colors, #301, 1957. Doll on left in blue print is not a Littlest Angel.*
Marilyn McDonald Collection,

***LANTERN DRESS.** Dress is #309 from 1957.*
Marilyn McDonald Collection.

***RAINCOAT AND HAT,** #413, 1957.*
Marilyn McDonald Collection.

***LITTLEST ANGEL.** Vinyl head, wearing **BROWN STRIPE DRESS,** #416 from 1957. Original box.*
Marilyn McDonald Collection.

**DENIM SMOCK, #503,
from 1957 catalog.**

Denim Smock
#503 . . . **$2.00**
Prices are for outfits only

**ICE SKATER, #509 from 1957
catalog.**

RED PLAID DRESS, #417, 1957.
Marilyn McDonald Collection.

ALICE in WONDERLAND, #517, 1957.
Marilyn McDonald Collection.

**GOLF OUTFIT, #519 from 1957; and ICE
SKATER, #058 from 1955.**
Marilyn McDonald Collection.

CARDIGAN AND HAT, #523, 1957.
Accessories not identified.
Marilyn McDonald Collection.

PLEATED SKIRT AND BLOUSE, #527, 1957.
Marilyn McDonald Collection.

TAFFETA PARTY DRESS,
#529, 1957. All original
doll, rare outfit.
Marilyn McDonald Collection.

FORMAL, #604 from 1957.
Marilyn McDonald Collection.

**LITTLEST ANGEL, with original clothes in trunk.
Vinyl head. NYLON DRESS, #611 from 1957.**
Diana Gibson Collection.

**Original outfits in trunk with LITTLEST ANGEL. Trunk
is the same as in the photo below.**
Diana Gibson Collection.

**Original trunk for LITTLEST ANGEL. Made of paperboard,
with colorful graphics, plastic handle, and corner guards.**
Private Collection.

LITTLEST ANGEL. Wearing NYLON DRESS, #611 from 1957.
Marilyn McDonald Collection.

EMBROIDERED DRESS, #618, 1957.
Marilyn McDonald Collection.

APPLIQUE DRESS, #619 from 1957.
Marilyn McDonald Collection.

SQUARE DANCE. Dress #620, 1957.
Marilyn McDonald Collection.

THREE-PIECE LEATHER JACKET, #623, 1957.

DOCTOR SCRUBS and 1957 ICE SKATER OUTFIT, #622.
Marilyn McDonald Collection.

FORMAL DRESS AND HAT, #707, 1957. *Marilyn McDonald Collection.*

Formal Dress
with Stole
#803 . . . **$4.00**

*FORMAL DRESS WITH STOLE,
#803, 1957 catalog.*

*VELVET COAT AND FORMAL GOWN, #804,
1957. Doll complete with wrist tag.*
Marilyn McDonald Collection.

*LITTLEST ANGEL in RED PRINT
DRESS, 1957 – 1958.*
Marilyn McDonald Collection.

*LITTLEST ANGEL. All original, felt jumper,
center snap shoes.*
Marilyn McDonald Collection.

*1958 brochure shows LITTLEST ANGEL with her new Dutch
Boy hair style. Brochure from the collection of Marge Meisinger. Photograph by Suzanne Silverthorn.*

Littlest Angel Transition Dolls

When Vogue purchased Arranbee in 1959, it carried the marked R&B Littlest Angel in an R&B box until 1963, but introduced her as a cousin in the Ginny family in 1961. For the transition Littlest Angel dolls of 1961 to 1963, see *Collector's Encyclopedia of Vogue Dolls* by Judith Izen and Carol Stover. Vogue also used the vinyl-headed Littlest Angel for its Little Imp doll. This version had orange hair, green eyes, and freckles, and was called "Brickette's Kid Sister." Note that the later Vogue Littlest Angel is a very different doll, made of all vinyl and having non-walking, straight legs.

LITTLEST ANGEL. Unusual long hair on this original doll, 1958(?).
Marilyn McDonald Collection.

FLOCKED PARTY DRESS and MATCHING BONNET. Rabbit fur jacket.
Marilyn McDonald Collection.

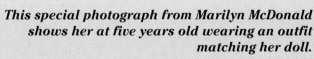

This special photograph from Marilyn McDonald shows her at five years old wearing an outfit matching her doll.

LITTLEST ANGEL WITH POLO COAT

A walking toddler doll with jointed body, knees that sit, walk and stand. Has vinyl head with rooted hair in dutch bob hair style. Dressed in camel hair polo coat with nautical brass buttons, red and white scarf tied around head, shoes and stockings. Height, 11 inches.

ST-46-1125 .... Each $5.00
Twelve in a shipping carton.

11" LITTLEST ANGEL. Hard plastic body, vinyl head with Dutch bob. 1959 Geo. Worthington Co. Wholesale Catalog.

LITTLEST ANGEL IN DUNGAREES

A walking toddler doll with jointed body and knees. Can sit, kneel, walk and stand. Has vinyl head with rooted hair do and dutch bob hair style. Dressed in knitted shirt and dungarees and matching shoes and socks. Height, 11 inches.

ST-46-1112 .... Each $4.00
Twelve in a shipping carton.

11" LITTLEST ANGEL. Dungaree outfit. 1959 Geo. Worthington Co. Wholesale Catalog.

LITTLEST ANGEL IN SCHOOL PINAFORE

A walking toddler doll with jointed body and knees that can sit, kneel, walk and stand. A vinyl head with rooted hair and dutch boy style hair do. Dressed in red dress with white pinafore with large schoolhouse on it, and ruffled edges. Also long red stockings and matching shoes. Height 11 inches.

ST-46-1123 .... Each $5.00
Twelve in a shipping carton.

11" LITTLEST ANGEL. The schoolhouse motif appears on various other Arranbee dolls, including Nanette. 1959 Geo. Worthington Co. Wholesale Catalog.

COUNTRY COUSIN. Vogue #4230, 1959. LI'L IMP, marked R&B 44. All original. Private Collection.

LITTLEST ANGEL BROWNIE SCOUT.
Marilyn McDonald Collection.

LITTLE IMP. 1960, marked R&B. Vogue #4161 DRESS AND PINAFORE outfit.
Marilyn McDonald Collection.

LITTLE IMP. This cute, original outfit matches the one on the 36" My Angel Walking Doll.
Marilyn McDonald Collection.

LITTLEST ANGEL. Vogue outfit #31261 from the 1961 Vogue catalog. Doll is marked R&B.
Marilyn McDonald Collection.

Fashion-of-the-Month

In 1955 and again in 1957, a special promotion was offered to children through various department stores: Littlest Angel Fashion-of-the-Month. A certificate was issued with membership, bearing the child's name, the giver, and the department store. The Certificate entitled the child to receive a different outfit for each month of the year. Although the outfits varied between the two years, they essentially followed the seasons. It must have seemed like a long wait for the child, as all the outfits were shown on the certificate and the child knew which one would come next. Note that the April Raincoat and December Deluxe Formal for 1955 are shown in previous photographs in this chapter. The 1957 outfits not shown are the January Teddy Bear Coat and the November Party Dress and Poodle.

FASHION OF THE MONTH. Cover from the 1955 flyer.

HALF-PRICE SPECIAL for Members Only!

"Littlest Angel" Doll
PLUS 3 Fashions
PLUS Steamer Trunk
for only $5

sold to non-members for $10

EVERY LITTLE GIRL wants to join in the fun! As a member in the "Littlest Angel" Fashion-of-the-Month Club, she receives the "Littlest Angel" doll, 3 beautiful fashions, a steamer trunk plus a new fashion every month for the *entire* year. Make her wish come true NOW! Enroll her in the most popular and exciting Club of the year!

IT'S SO EASY! All you do is fill out the coupon on the reverse side.

IT WORKS LIKE THIS: We immediately send your favorite little angel the exciting $10 gift package and an official membership certificate ready for framing. You will be charged the special price of only $5.00. Each month, for the next 12 months, she will receive the fashion of the month, as illustrated and on the membership certificate. The cost of each outfit will automatically be charged to you monthly.

The Club celebrity is "Littlest Angel" herself . . .
America's most popular doll!

Inside of the 1955 flyer showing the various monthly outfits.

1955 LITTLEST ANGEL FASHION OF THE MONTH CLUB certificate.
Diana Gibson Collection.

JANUARY — Pleated Dress.
Fur coat and hat added.
Marilyn McDonald Collection.

**Roller Skating Set
062 . . . $2.49**
Roller skating? With my jointed knees I'm a skating demon.
And my real denim overalls,
complete to the gold rivets
and red stitching, are guaranteed tumble-resistant. Complete with bright plaid blouse
and roller skates.

MARCH — Roller Skater.

**Rain Coat
046 . . . $1.49**
Stormy days aren't hard to
take at all. Fact is I almost
like them when I wear my
rugged red plastic rain coat,
with the belted waist. The
hood protects my just-combed
Saran curls.

APRIL — Raincoat.

FEBRUARY — Plaid Dress.
Private Collection.

JUNE — Bridal Outfit.
Private Collection.

MAY — Sunsuit.
Diana Gibson Collection.

Beach Apparel
052 . . . $1.98
Recognize me behind dark glasses? I'm a real sun-beauty in my hooded yellow robe (which I made sure **didn't** cover my new jointed knees). Colorful 2-piece swim suit has matching bag and sandals.

JULY — Beach Outfit.

Riding Habit
067 . . . $2.49
I don't need help mounting my pony now that I can bend my knees. I'm off to the hunt in my bright red gold-buttoned vest, stunning white jodhpurs, jaunty red cap and riding boots.

AUGUST — Riding Habit.

SEPTEMBER — School Dress.
Marilyn McDonald Collection.

Sailor
045 . . . $1.49
Set for a day of yachting, I'm wearing a white pique dress with nautical designs, and sailor's collar trimmed with naval stars. My sailor's cap sports a plump pom-pom.

OCTOBER — Sailor Outfit.

Coat, Hat, Dress
033 . . . $2.98
For holiday time, I wear a stylish hat and coat with matching lace trim on the coat's wide collar and hat. Underneath I'm wearing a pretty, Christmassy dress.

NOVEMBER — Coat, Hat, Dress. Marilyn McDonald Collection.

Ice Skater
#509 . . . **$2.00**

FEBRUARY — Ice Skater.
1957 Fashion of the Month.

MARCH — Sailor Dress.

Rain Outfit
#413 . . . **$1.50**

APRIL — Raincoat.

MAY — Nylon Dress.
Diana Gibson Collection.

JUNE — Bride.
Marilyn McDonald Collection.

**Tennis Ensemble
041 . . . $1.49**
Sure I play tennis! Get around
the court wonderfully with my
jointed knees. I attract loads
of attention with my colorful
three-piece print outfit, removable skirt, matching visor.
My own tennis racket, too.

JULY — Tennis outfit
with racket.

**TV Lounging Clothes
066 . . . $2.49**
I've an evening of televiewing in mind, so I've slipped into this handsome, mustard-colored at-home costume, made complete by a luxurious red bolero jacket trimmed in rich gold.

AUGUST — TV Outfit.

*SEPTEMBER — SCHOOL DRESS AND
HAT SET, #526, 1957.*
Private Collection.

Square Dancer
#620 . . . **$2.50**

OCTOBER — Square Dancer.

DECEMBER — Coat, Hat, Dress.

Sweet Pea

Sweet Pea, billed as Littlest Angel's baby sister, was highlighted at the Arranbee showroom during the 1955 Toy Fair. An 11" baby, she was made of all vinyl with rooted hair and sleeping eyes. Details of both her body and her head were very realistic, and she even had individual toes. She could drink and wet, and came dressed in a diaper, with baby bottle; her layette consisted of 15 different baby outfits that were designed for easy removal by a child. By 1957, many more outfits were available for her.

June 1955 advertisement in **Playthings** *for the Mickey Mouse Club promotion.*

1955 SWEET PEA brochure.

SWEET PEA. This one has straight hair. Arms and legs have lost their original color.

SWEET PEA. All vinyl body construction with well-defined details. This is a high-quality baby doll.

2-pc. Sleeper 201 . . . $.98
Give Sweet Pea her bottle at bed time and she'll fall asleep quickly. For what could be more comfortable, or better to dream in, than this 2-piece sleeper that slips on so easily.

#201 SLEEPER for SWEET PEA. Matches Littlest Angel.

Print Dress 202 . . . $.98
There's a filmy net covering bodice of this perfect afternoon frock. Buttons and lace trim are in keeping with the saucy flower print and whirling skirt.

#202 PRINT DRESS.

Striped Sunsuit 203 . . . $.98
She's tres chic (and so daring!) in this candy-striped bare-back sun suit. Slim straps are satin, and tie pertly around the neck. Note open-toed sandals.

#203 STRIPED SUN-SUIT. Matches a Littlest Angel outfit.

Checked Sun Suit 211 . . . $1.49
Sweet Pea is all set for a place in the sun in panty-bottom checked sun suit. Wide brim bonnet and open-toed sandals for real relaxation.

#211 CHECKED SUN SUIT. Coordinates with a Littlest Angel outfit.

**Terry Cloth Outfit
212 . . . 1.49**
Finished with her tub, Sweet Pea climbs into long slacks and loose fitting pull-over, both in comfortable terry cloth. Frisky animal figure on blouse front, tassle-rope forms bow at the neck. Terry cloth scuffs.

#212 TERRY CLOTH OUTFIT.

**Blanket and Robe
213 . . . $1.49**
Wrapped in her snug fitting blanket, Sweet Pea is ready for her bottle, and for dozing off in mommy's arms. The bathrobe is white with tiny sprinkles of flowers, ties at the waist.

#213 BLANKET AND ROBE.

**Garbardine Bunting
221 . . . $1.98**
Sweet Pea doesn't shiver on cold days. Zippered up in her gabardine bunting, she faces the meanest change in the weather. Complete with warm cap and mittens.

*#221 GABARDINE BUNTING.
See a similar bunting on
Angel Face in Chapter 12.*

**Corduroy Romper
222 . . . $1.98**
Even a darling like Sweet Pea wants to rough it sometimes, and this practical romper, of hardy corduroy, stands up under any treatment. Two big buttons and animal figure decorate the costume.

#222 CORDUROY ROMPER.

**Taffeta Dress
223 . . . $1.98**
The envy of the bunting crowd in this really exquisite taffeta party dress. Delicately embroidered flowers at the hem. Tight fitting bodice, flare skirt. Lacy matching bonnet.

#223 TAFFETA DRESS.

**Nylon Dress
231 . . . $2.49**
This sweet little nylon frock, with full skirt, is as easy to wash as Sweet Pea herself. Bright, fresh and lacy, it's so appropriate for almost any occasion. Matching bonnet.

#231 NYLON DRESS.

**Pinafore Outfit
232 . . . $2.49**
Sweet Pea stays cool on hot days in this dainty organdy pinafore. Flower at the waist, zig-zag trim along the full skirt, and lace over the shoulders. Matching bonnet.

#232 PINAFORE OUTFIT.

**Pram Set
233 . . . $2.49**
What royal elegance! Sweet Pea's fur-trimmed pram set. white fur at the wrists and on bonnet to outline her baby face. Sleeves button into mittens. Zips up for real warmth.

#233 PRAM SET.

**Coat Outfit
241 . . . $2.98**
How proud Sweet Pea is, going bye-bye in her stunning taffeta coat. High styled simplicity is the keynote—lace trim on collar and bonnet add dash of adornment.

#241 COAT OUTFIT Coordinates with Littlest Angel.

**Sweater and Dress
242 . . . $2.98**
No more appropriate traveling outfit for Sweet Pea than this sturdy but feminine sweater and dress combination. The sweater's rocky weave contrasts with full skirt, through which we peep at a pretty petticoat.

#242 SWEATER OUTFIT.

**Christening Dress
243 . . . $2.98**
What a charming picture Sweet Pea makes outfitted in this long-flowing white Christening dress. So delicate and beautiful, it has an embroidered column along the extra wide skirt, bow at the waist. Bonnet to match.

#243 CHRISTENING DRESS.

#2200 CRADLE.

12" SWEET PEA. 1955. *All vinyl drink-and-wet baby with realistic details throughout; rooted hair. Marked R&B. Original box covered with graphics. All original, with baby bottle. Promoted as Littlest Angel's baby sister.*
Marilyn McDonald Collection.

1957 SWEET PEA brochure.

1957 outfits: #207 201, 206, 205.

1957 outfits: #215, 218, 217, 216.

Pink Dot
Organdy Dress
#215 . . . **$1.50**

Flannel Blanket
and Robe Set
#218 . . . **$1.50**

Quilted Robe
#217 . . . **$1.50**

Organdy Dress
#216 . . . **$1.50**

1957 outfits: #228, 226, 227.

Maize Organdy Dress
#228 . . . **$2.00**

Jingle Slacks
#226 . . . **$2.00**

Pink Organdy Dress
#227 . . . **$2.00**

1957 outfits: #236, 238, 237.

White Nylon Dress
#236 . . . **$2.50**

Pink Nylon Dress
#238 . . . **$2.50**

Blue Nylon Dress
#237 . . . **$2.50**

| Toe-Length Dress and Jacket Outfit #247 . . . **$3.00** | Coat, Hat and Dress Outfit #246 . . . **$3.00** | Nylon Christening Dress Outfit #248 . . . **$3.00** | Knitted Sweater and Dress Set #245 . . . **$3.00** |

1957 outfits: #247, 246, 248, 245.

NOW...Cries Real Tears!

Sweet Pea

Littlest Angel's Baby Sister. For ages 3 to 10 years.

ENDLESS HOURS OF PLAYTIME PLEASURE FOR HER LITTLE MOTHER!

The sweetheart of all baby dolls, Sweet Pea stands a full 12 inches, drinks and wets, and is all-vinyl. She has moving eyes and her lustrous hair is rooted in— can't be pulled out! She comes complete with diapers, plastic diaper cover, booties and bottle. Like Littlest Angel, Sweet Pea has a wide range of separate outfits to choose from . . . in gift boxes. From $1.00 to $4.00

#2010 As Shown . . . $3⁹⁸

Back cover of 1957 brochure.

April Showers and Lil' Cupcake

Since April Showers and Lil' Cupcake appeared near the end of Arranbee's history, they are therefore among the company's more elusive dolls. Measuring 11", they are made of soft vinyl with molded hair, and have sleeping eyes and nursing mouths. The markings on their heads are very faint or missing altogether, so their name tags are the only identification.

A note on credits:

1954 flyer reprints are from the authors' collection.
1955 catalog reprints are from the authors' collection.
1957 catalog reprints are from Marilyn McDonald's collection. Other credits as given with photographs.

LIL' CUPCAKE. Faint markings on the back of her head. Original pajama outfit, shoes, and socks. The yellow dress and bonnet actually belong to Sweet Pea. $85.00.

Ad for APRIL SHOWERS, October 1957 Playthings. She has molded hair, and came with a tub, shower, and bathing accessories. The April Showers name is not found in later advertisements.

Closeup of LIL CUPCAKE.

Original box for LIL' CUPCAKE.

Arranbee Fashion Dolls
Coty Girl and Nanette

Coty Girl

The late 1950's saw the arrival of many small 9" to 11" fashion type dolls, with feet molded for high-heeled shoes. The quality of these dolls varied greatly, with many of them being marked with a *P* in a circle. In 1957, Arranbee introduced its 10" Coty Girl, which used one of the *P* in a circle models. Having a body very similar to Little Miss Revlon with its jointed waist, Coty Girl was a top-of-the-line doll, and is not to be confused with other *P* in a circle marked dolls of lesser quality. She had long, thick, rooted hair which could easily be washed and styled; painted lashes (which similar dolls do not have) are another Coty Girl characteristic. Popular since she was first produced, she is difficult for the new collector to identify without original clothes or box, or without knowing her particular characteristics. As a result, other small fashions dolls are sometimes erroneously advertised as Coty dolls.

Coty Girl was a registered trademark of Coty, Div. of Pfizer, and the doll was used to promote the Coty cosmetics. Coty Girl was so popular that in 1958 Arranbee promoted her extensively in several media, including March 1 and 15th appearances on NBC's *Ruff and Ready* television show — and that is why the cover of the brochure, showing her many outfits, pictures her on a television screen wearing her signature black, saw-toothed hat.

> *Prices for Coty Girl:*
>
> Mint nude doll: $125.00+ (add more with box).
> Played with nude dolls: $35.00 – 45.00.
> Outfits: $35.00 – 45.00 (boxed) or $10.00 – 25.00.
> (played with).

1957 COTY GIRL advertisement.

10" COTY GIRL. 1958 General Merchandise catalog.

1958 R&B catalog showing Coty Girl fashions.
From the collection of Marge Meisinger; photograph by Suzanne Silverthorn.

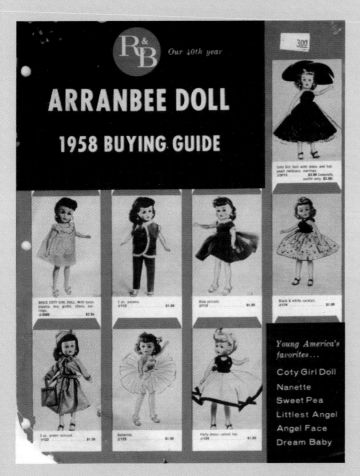

1958 R&B catalog showing Coty Girl fashions.
From the collection of Marge Meisinger; photograph by Suzanne Silverthorn.

This is outfit #120, PICNIC DRESS.
Coty Dickson Collection.

10" COTY GIRL. Basic doll in original box, with hang tag. Her lingerie is exactly like that on the 18" Nanette fashion bride, both in design and material.
Coty Dickson Collection.

Rain Outfit
#122 . . . **$1.50**
Includes Rain Hat
and Shoes

Outfit #122, RAIN OUTFIT.

Negligee Outfit
#130 . . . **$2.00**
Includes Shoes

Outfit #130, NEGLIGEE.

COTY GIRL wearing #131, WOOL SHRUG.
Coty Dickson Collection.

Another type of original box for COTY GIRL. Doll is wearing BLUE STRIPE DRESS, #133.
Coty Dickson Collection.

COTY GIRL wearing outfit #134, SWIM SUIT AND CAPE. Other outfits are: TULLE FORMAL, #157; TOREADOR, #146; and DRESS AND WOOL SHRUG, #131.
Coty Dickson Collection.

COTY GIRL and 1957 gift box. The gift box contained three outfits: SQUARE DANCING, #145; TULLE FORMAL, #157; and PICNIC DRESS, #120.
Coty Dickson Collection.

Cocktail Party Dress
#143 . . . **$2.50**
Includes Jeweled Pin, Crystal
Earrings and Shoes

Outfit #143, COCKTAIL PARTY.

Tailored Suit and Blouse
#144 . . . **$2.50**
Includes Shoulder Length Bag,
Crystal Earrings, Straw Hat
and Shoes
Prices are for outfits and accessories only!

*Outfit #144, TAILORED SUIT
AND BLOUSE.*

*This ultra fashionable COTY GIRL is
wearing outfit #134, SWIM SUIT AND
CAPE. Swimsuit has a Dolphin motif on
lower left side. Outfit is complete, with
matching beach bag, sunglasses, and
straw hat.* Coty Dickson Collection.

*Brunette COTY GIRL wearing
SQUARE DANCE DRESS (#145) in red,
with original red shoes. A version of
this dress can be seen on Littlest
Angel.* Coty Dickson Collection.

*Blond COTY GIRL wearing SQUARE
DANCE DRESS (#145) in blue, with black
heels. Both this doll and the preceding
wear original pearl earrings and neck-
laces.* Coty Dickson Collection .

*TOREADOR outfit (#146)
on brunette COTY GIRL.
Pearl earrings replace her
original crystal ones.*
Coty Dickson Collection.

Bridal Outfit
#156 . . . **$3.00**

Includes Pearl Necklace, Blue
Garter and Shoes

Outfit #156, BRIDAL OUTFIT.

COTY GIRL wearing
TULLE FORMAL (#157),
complete with velvet
high-heel shoes. This
outfit originally came
with a jeweled pin and
crystal earrings.
Coty Dickson Collection.

Denim Play Outfit
#158 . . . **$3.00**

Includes Straw Hat, Gold Earrings,
Gold Bracelet, Sun Glasses and Shoes

Outfit #158, DENIM PLAY OUTFIT.

Velvet Wrap and Formal
#171 . . . **$5.00**

Includes Crystal Necklace, Crystal Drop
Earrings, Nylon Stockings and Shoes

Outfit #171, VELVET WRAP
AND FORMAL.

Not all the outfits available for Coty Girl are shown. Other outfits available include:

#112, Pajamas.

#114, Black and White Cocktail Dress. Black halter top, white skirt with black design.

#121, Cowl Neck Dress. Light blue, with diamond print and pink cowl neck.

#124, Sleeveless Party Dress. Black velvet top, white skirt with black trim, and small bows at the hem.

#126, Brown Dress and Hat.

#132, Gingham Check Dress, with straw bag.

#136, Print Cotton Dress. Puffed sleeves; bonnet.

#138, Graduation Gown. Includes a mortar board with tassel and a diploma.

#151, Leather Car Coat. Light color with stripes; scarf and handbag, and black and white checked slacks.

#153, Coat, Hat, and Muff. Simulated lamb's skin.

Nanette Fashion Doll

Arranbee's larger fashion dolls bore the Nanette name, but these dolls were a dramatic change from the earlier Nanettes, both in style and material. The first model, in 1958, resembled the Ideal Miss Revlon doll, both in construction and appearance, with a swivel waist and feet that were molded to wear high-heeled shoes. The clothes on both dolls are easily interchangeable. By 1959, however, the Nanette fashion dolls were made with a plastic body and soft vinyl head; although of lesser quality, their clothes were just as fashionable, with many glamorous outfits available. Few of these larger fashion dolls appear today, as they were produced for only a very short time. Many of them are unmarked and are difficult to identify if found nude. Some have been seen with a *V* and a number, which represents a Valentine Doll mold.

A rare version of the Nanette doll is the 18" Coty Girl Deluxe, although the other Nanette fashions came in two sizes: 15" and 18", with the first two digits on the outfit number indicating the doll's size. Nanette was also available in a trunk in just the 15" size: one as a bride in a display box with extra outfits, and the other in afternoon dress with extra outfits. Several of the Nanette outfits are almost identical (or at least similar) to those found on the smaller Coty Girl.

We did not find enough examples of Nanette fashion dolls to determine a realistic price range.

1958 R&B catalog showing available NANETTE fashion outfits. From the collection of Marge Meisinger, photograph by Suzanne Silverthorn.

18" NANETTE BRIDE. Original BRIDAL OUTFIT, #1806. A Nanette wrist tag came on this doll, but it does not appear in this photograph. Courtesy of Delores Delgado.

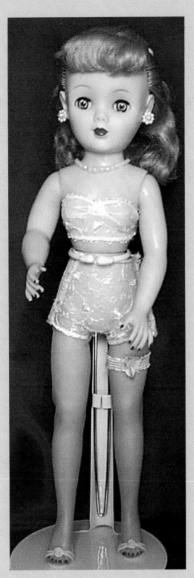

Under garments on 18" NANETTE. This doll very closely resembles Ideal's Miss Revlon in her body construction.

15" BRIDE DOLL with TROUSSEAU. 1959 Geo. Worthington Co. Wholesale Catalog.

BRIDE DOLLS

All vinyl girl doll with high heels, swivel waist and rooted hair. Dressed in beautiful bride's outfit that includes a crinoline slip, satin gown, nylon lace overskirt, flower bouquet and veil of lace trimmed with flowers. Also includes bra, girdle, pearl earrings, necklace and ring. Height, 18 inches. Weight per shipping carton, 25 lbs.

ST-46-1806 ———————————————— **Each $10.00**

18" BRIDE DOLL. From the 1959 Geo. Worthington Co. Wholesale Catalog.

BRIDE WITH TROUSSEAU

All vinyl girl doll with high-heeled shoes, swivel waist and rooted hair. Dressed in a bride's out-fit that includues a crinoline slip, satin gown, nylon lace overskirt, flower bouquet, veil of lace trimmed with flowers and bra and girdle under-neath. Also includes nylon negligee, blue taffeta dress with red satin bow trim, handbag contain-ing rhinestone necklace and earrings, red straw hat and 2 pairs of shoes. Complete with carry-ing case. Doll height, 15 inches. Weight per shipping carton, 54 lbs.

ST-46-6500 ———————————————— **Each $15.00**

Yellow print dress for the 18"
Nanette fashion doll. It originally
came with a solid yellow shrug and
black heels. The complete outfit is
MAIZE SHRUG, #1804.
$28.83, internet auction.

*18" NANETTE, 1958 fashion doll. This outfit is
#1809, COTILLION-MAIZE. Rigid plastic body has
the unusual feature of jointed wrists; head is
vinyl, with rooted hair. High fashion styling on
gown: yellow floral nylon over yellow taffeta
with black velvet and lace trim. Black velvet cape
is lined in yellow, with a rhinestone studded self
bow. Rhinestones also adorn her gown, as well as
her earrings, necklace, and bracelet. Marked
R&B on box; doll has no markings.*

View of 18" NANETTE FASHION without her cape.

Face and bodice details of 18" NANETTE FASHION. This doll was produced about the time Vogue purchased Arranbee and reflects the industry change to a lighter, less expensive material.

18" COTY GIRL DELUXE. This rare doll is actually the larger version of the 11" Coty Girl, but she appears in the Nanette fashion brochure as part of that line. Truly high fashion in her black tulle and satin dress, signature Coty Girl hat, high heel shoes, and nylon stockings with embroidered front. Original R&B box. Internet auction, $352.00.
Courtesy of Loren E. Miller.

Closer view of COTY GIRL DELUXE.
Courtesy of Loren E. Miller.

By 1950, Arranbee was adding various dolls to their lines which were made with a new, soft material called vinyl (or vinylite). During the 1950's and later, it was also used extensively throughout the doll industry for heads with rooted hair on both the hard plastic and all vinyl bodies. The first vinyl heads, however, had the usual glued-on wigs. Some of the very earliest vinyl tended to seep an oily residue that is difficult to remove today. As the process of manufacturing of this material was perfected, however, this problem was soon overcome. Rarely encountered on Arranbee dolls, it appears mainly on lesser quality dolls.

Nanette

The Nanette name was continued on the vinyl head/hard plastic body version, but the face on this later doll is wider and squarer than the one on the hard plastic head. Some of this appearance can be attributed to too warm a temperature, which further softened the vinyl and caused the head to settle on the neck. This problem can sometimes be solved by stuffing the head with cotton, not an easy project but worth it for an otherwise nice doll.

There are two different kinds of walker bodies on these Nanette dolls with the vinyl heads. First is the regular body, with an added walker mechanism that includes a rod extending up into the head so that the doll's head moves as she walks. The other walker body has pin joints at the sides of the hips. Both of these models were available with or without knee joints.

22

NANETTE

R & B's Popular Walking Girl Doll! With Jointed Knees, Rooted Saran Hair, Vinyl Head   From $7.98 up

NANETTE — With a gleam in her eye and a spring in her step, Nanette is a typical little girl — and always a happy companion. Nanette walks right along with her older girl friends, and as she walks, she turns her head from side to side, so she won't miss a trick! She stands, sits down, and opens and closes her eyes. Her beautiful, long Saran hair can be washed and set in the latest style, and no matter where she goes or what she does, Nanette's guaranteed not to crack, peel or chip.

Nanette comes in a variety of slip-on costumes and is available in little girl sizes: 15", 18", 25" (and a life-size 30", as shown in detail in next section of this booklet).

Short Party Dress
7215, 15"—$7.98; 7218, 18"—$9.98; 7225, 25"—$14.98
A jumper effect accents crisp white blouse with puffed sleeves. Belt at waist sits atop an unusually flare skirt which sports flower and stripe design. Crinoline slip, hair ribbon and matching tote bag.

Cover of NANETTE 1955 brochure, showing outfit #7215, SHORT PARTY DRESS, with matching tote bag. Other sizes available, but with different numbers. Nanette has a vinyl head with rooted Saran hair.

Prices are for outfits only.

School Girl
7115, 15" — $ 7.98
7118, 18" — $ 9.98
7125, 25" — $14.98

Nanette's a striking figure in this pert "sailor" school dress. A whistle is tied to snappy cord belt. Naval stars adorn the front of a wide skirt. Wide white collar sports sailboat designs.

Outfit #7115, SCHOOL GIRL. Other sizes available with different numbers.

15" Nanette Ballerina, Metal Wardrobe Trunk
7300 — $14.98

15" Nanette comes dressed in her graceful ballerina outfit, along with several costume changes for all occasions, in this compact metal trunk. Clothes fit perfectly, and are on hangers. Extra shoes, roller skates, sun glasses.

Outfit #7300, 15" BALLERINA, in case with extra clothes.

Ballerina
7315, 15" — $7.98
7318, 18" — $9.98

A spray of tiny buds — in her hair, entwined with net about the neck, and in her hand — the finishing touches for Nanette's graceful satin-top net-bottom ballet costume. Anklet-tied slippers.

Outfit #7315, 15" BALLERINA. 18" size is numbered 7318.

Coat and Hat
7515, 15" — $ 8.98
7518, 18" — $11.98
7525, 25" — $16.98

Nanette's dress coat has a form-fitted, double-breasted top — then loosens into eye-catching flare. Smart white sloping collar and wide cuffs contain dashing stripe. Afternoon dress beneath. Pompomed beret.

Outfit #7515, 15" COAT AND HAT. 18" and 25" sizes have different numbers.

Net Formal
7615, 15" — $ 8.98
7618, 18" — $11.98
7625, 25" — $17.98

No smarter formal than this net masterpiece. Satin underskirt enhances billowing net for a very full effect. Satin bows, flower trimmed, on the skirt. Stand-up neckline and puffed sleeves. Note that the skirt is over-all embroidered.

Outfit #7615, 15" NET FORMAL. 18" and 25" have different numbers.

15″ Nanette Bride, Metal Wardrobe Trunk

7700 — $17.98

15″ Nanette dressed as a bride fits perfectly, along with her trousseau, in this well made metal trunk, which shuts securely and is easy to carry. Trousseau includes dress, sports outfit, extra shoes, roller skates, sun glasses.

Outfit #7700, 15″ BRIDE AND TRUNK. Metal trunk carries her trousseau.

Outfit #7715, 15″ BRIDE. 18″ and 25″ have different numbers.

Bride

7715, 15″ — $ 9.98
7718, 18″ — $12.98
7725, 25″ — $19.98

Nanette's wedding! She wears exquisite satin-net gown. Delicate flower petals stand between the skirt's satin and net bottom. Satin hat surrounded by flowers and illusion net veil. She wears pearls, carries old fashioned bouquet.

Fur Cape

7915, 15″ — $11.98
7918, 18″ — $14.98

Net and lace formal(previously described) highlights the elegance of this white fur cape, which hugs the shoulders and only partially hides Nanette's arms. Fastens high on the throat.

Outfit #7915, FUR CAPE for 15″ doll. Separate item to wear with Net Formal. 18″ has number 7918.

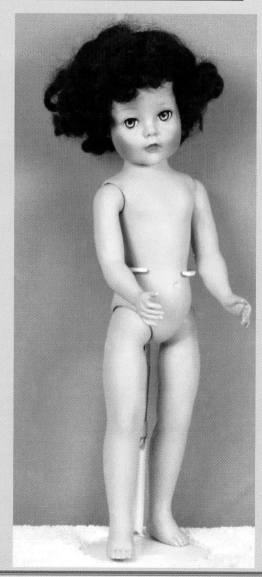

Body construction of vinyl head Nanette.

14" NANETTE. Hard plastic, with early vinyl head marked Arranbee. Glued on blond wig and sleeping eyes. Original green and white dress; plastic shoes marked Fairyland. $85.00.

17" NANETTE. Vinyl head marked Arranbee. Same body as found on hard plastic Nanette. Brunette wig is glued on, not rooted. Appropriately redressed. $89.00.

18" DREAM BRIDE. Hard plastic walker with jointed knees; vinyl head is marked R&B. Glued on brown wig. Tiered gown and chapel cap; white satin shoes. $150.00.

17" NANETTE WALKER. *Hard plastic with vinyl head. Mint doll is all original, with original navy coat and hat. This is outfit #7515, as shown in 1955 brochure.* Dorothy Feingold Collection.

Back view of 17" NANETTE.

Dress on 17" NANETTE.

Head detail of 17" NANETTE.

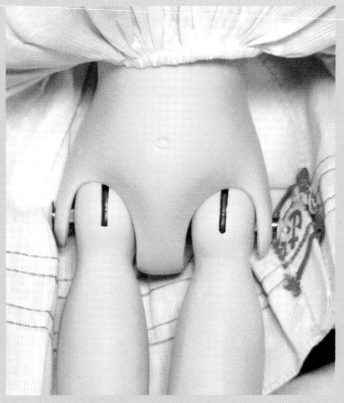

Details of hips and knees on 17" NANETTE.

Wrist tag front.

IT'S EASY AND SO MUCH
FUN TO GIVE ME A NEW
HAIR-DO!

Moisten the hair lightly with
water—Set hair in curlers. When
hair is dry remove curlers. Very
simple indeed.

You'll love these
R&B dolls:

Littlest Angel   Nanette
Sweet Pea   Angel Skin
Angel Face   Dream Baby

Wrist tag reverse side.

LIFE-SIZE
NANETTE

Best of All! Sweet Nanette In The Life-Size 30"!

From $19.98

Just imagine a lovely walking girl doll 2½ feet tall! Why, she's actually a friend to any little girl. Life-sized Nanette has all the features of the small Nanette — all plastic body that won't chip, crack or peel, walks, has jointed knees, sits, stands, moves vinyl head from side to side, moving eyes for waking or sleep, and the same wonderful rooted Saran hair that can be washed, combed, and curled. And, she's a full 30"! Not just a show doll, but one your little girl will play with constantly. Available, from $19.98, in four beautiful costumes.

1955 booklet for Life-Size NANETTE.

30" Short Party Dress
7230 — $19.98

30" of little lady, Nanette wears her party dress. Big puff sleeves with satin bow. White blouse top contrasts with silky full skirt. Crinoline petticoat. Costume is coordinated by matching pocketbook and wide belt.

Outfit #7230, PARTY DRESS.

30" Coat and Hat
7530 — $21.98

Nanette's tiny waist is sharply emphasized in this double-breasted full-bottom coat. A bold pom-pom is featured on matching beret. Smart street dress underneath. And Nanette stands a big 30" tall!

Outfit #7530, COAT AND HAT.

30" Net Formal
7630 — $23.98

A majestic 30" tall, Nanette's a princess in this beautiful over-all embroidered net creation. Graceful stand-up collar. Satin ribbon bows, flower trimmed, rest gently on the skirt. The waves of net cover hooped satin skirt.

Outfit #7630, NET FORMAL.

30" Bride
7730 — $24.98

Ultimate in beautiful dolls — 30" Bride Nanette! Gown of bridal satin and net, decorated with flower petals around skirt, neckline, and around satin hat. Net veiling. Satin top is encased in net, with net sleeves. Nanette wears a strand of pearls, carries an old fashioned bouquet.

Outfit #7730, BRIDE.

Taffy

Taffy was a departure from Arranbee's usual line of pretty-face girl dolls. Having a face reminiscent of Alexander's Cissy, Taffy was more of a character doll, with turned-up nose, a wide face, and an almost chirping look to her mouth. Unfortunately, a characteristic of this doll is that the soft vinyl head has a tendency to settle on the neck of her hard plastic body, which alters her cute appearance.

18" TAFFY. Hard plastic walker body; vinyl head marked 18ARV R&B. All original: royal blue taffeta skirt attached to blue flocked blouse, stretch belt with flowers, separate half slip. $135.00.

18" TAFFY. All original, with walker body and vinyl head. This peasant style outfit can also be seen on the hard plastic Nanette. Marilyn McDonald Collection.

Back view of 18" Taffy.

Closeup of 25" TAFFY.

25" TAFFY. Vinyl head marked ARV25 R&B; rooted golden blond hair. Hard plastic walker body, with grill in chest and straight legs. Lavender taffeta dress has gold diamond pattern; not original. Original gold snap-front shoes. $110.00.

Hip construction on 25" TAFFY.

Nancy Lee Toddler

In the early 1950's, the hard plastic Nancy Lee was no longer offered; in its place was a 16" (can measure 15") vinyl toddler doll with the same name. Marked Arranbee, she had chubby limbs and torso, and was rather heavy. Her face was very distinctive with its wavy eyebrows and big eyes. Being one of the very first all vinyl dolls that Arranbee produced, she had a glued-on wig. She appears infrequently today at doll shows and auctions, and rarely with original clothing, indicating that she was likely very popular with children.

ADVERTISED IN **LIFE**

New chubby doll with budget appeal...

Nancy Lee

All vinylite. Hair that can be washed, combed and curled. Regular or "rooted" wig. Retail from $9.98. Separate garments to retail at $2.98.

BRAND NEW, chubby Nancy Lee is all vinylite, washable from "head to toe". Sell her "undressed"—wearing slip, shoes and socks—and make extra sales of separate clothes, designed just for her. Buyers report average sale of 3 garments per doll.

This is just one of the many promotional items in the new Arranbee line. Backed by vigorous advertising in LIFE—one-half page November 3rd and one-half page November 17th—pre-selling 20,000,000 readers. See your Arranbee salesman now and be prepared to cash in on this demand.

1952 advertisement in **Playthings** *for the vinylite Nancy Lee doll.*

Advertisement from unknown magazine showing Nancy Lee.

Give life-like "Nancy Lee," made of VINYLITE Brand Plastics

R & B's Nancy Lee is pretty as a picture! And her little mother is going to love cuddling her . . . washing her soft, natural-feeling face and body . . . washing, combing and curling her flowing hair. And, being made of VINYLITE Brand Resins from her head to her delicately molded toes, she won't crack, dent, peel or break when maternal care is none too gentle.

Many, many other things of everyday life are made better thanks to these versatile resins. There are dish drainers that don't get soggy, floor coverings that seal out dirt, to name but two. You can always count on excellent performance when you spot that VINYLITE trade-mark. Look for it!

14" NANCY LEE TODDLER. Marked Arranbee. Glued on blond Saran wig in original set. All original. Wrist tag has attached curlers to set her hair. Never played with doll. $175.00.

14" NANCY LEE TODDLER. 1952 chubby vinyl child with glued-on brown wig. Original flocked nylon gown, taffeta half slip, body suit, and black shoes that snap in front. Ribbons not original. $95.00.

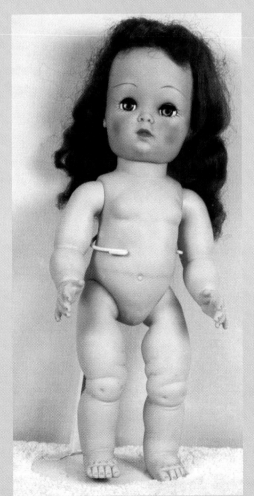

Body construction of 14" NANCY LEE TODDLER.

14" NANCY LEE TODDLER. Marked Arranbee. All original, but one shoe is missing.
Annette Davino Collection.

14" NANCY LEE TODDLER. Blond wig and appropriate re-dressing. *Patricia Snyder Collection.*

NANCY LEE IN SCHOOL PINAFORE

All vinyl toddler doll with five piece jointed body, vinyl head with dutch bob hair style. Doll is dressed in red dress with red and white checked pinafore with school house on it, shoes and socks. Height, 14 inches.

ST-46-1402 .... Each $5.00
Twelve in a shipping carton.

14" NANCY LEE. 1959 toddler has a different face from the preceding year's doll. She also has a Dutch bob. The schoolhouse motif appears on the dresses of several different Arranbee dolls. Geo. Worthington Co. Wholesale Catalog.

NANCY LEE IN DUNGAREES

All vinyl toddler doll with five piece jointed body, and vinyl head with dutch bob hair style. Doll is dressed in red tee shirt, dungarees, shoes and socks. Height 14 inches.

ST-46-1412 .... Each $5.00
Twelve in a shipping carton.

14" NANCY LEE. Another toddler from the preceding catalog.

Vinyl Babies, Little Girl Dolls, and Teen Agers

Vinyl's characteristic softness made a more appealing material for the baby and little girl dolls, and Arranbee made a great variety of them. This new material offered seemingly unlimited possibilities for head and body construction. Since many of these Arranbee vinyl dolls were produced in the late 1950's, a number of them were carried over into the Arranbee/Vogue period. Collectors will also note the resemblance between several of these dolls and the Vogue dolls of the early 1960's.

F Arranbee Angel Face Doll. Chubby all-vinyl 20" toddler with fully jointed arms and legs. She drinks and wets, has moving eyes, rooted hair. Her nylon dress has a checked petticoat. Ages 3 to 10. (#20822) **7.95**

20" ANGEL FACE. Mid-1950 advertisement in Paris Fair *catalog. All vinyl, with rooted hair; a fully washable baby doll, available in four sizes up to 25".*

28

ANGEL FACE
Darling Moulded Vinyl Baby Doll   From $5.98

Despite her angelic and delicate appearance, Angel Face isn't hurt by those inevitable accidents, because she's vinyl from head to toe. That makes her completely washable, too. She's especially appealing with her moving eyes and cooing voice.

Available in four popular sizes: 16", 19", 22", and 25" in a fetching variety of bunting or dress outfits. From $5.98 up. With painted hair, or rooted Saran hair that can be combed, washed, and curled.

Nylon Dress	
5416, 16" —	$ 7.98
5419, 19" —	$ 8.98
5422, 22" —	$ 9.98
5425, 25" —	$12.98

Fine embroidery catches your eye first on this adorable nylon baby dress. Like all baby outfits it has full and flowing lines. Lace-and-ruffles bonnet covers Angel Face's rooted Saran hair.

1955 Brochure for ANGEL FACE.

Angel Face GABARDINE BUNTING.

Gabardine Bunting
5219, 19" — $ 8.98
5222, 22" — $ 9.98
5225, 25" — $11.98

Angel Face, here with rooted Saran hair, is warmly dressed against winter winds in this zip-up gabardine bunting. V-shaped floral pattern across the front. Muffler and mittens have identical design. Pom-pom atop cozy hat.

Angel Face COAT AND HAT.

22" Coat and Hat
5522 — $12.98

Angel Face wears a flare corduroy coat for dress up occasions. White applique along collar and cuffs. Button down front. Frilly baby bonnet ties in satin bow under chin. Dainty dress and petticoat under coat.

Fleece- Bunting

5319, 19″ — $ 9.98
5322, 22″ — $10.98
5325, 25″ — $12.98

Angel Face couldn't possibly be warmer than in this fleece bunting, especially when it zips right up under the chin. Note gay stripe effect. In contrasting color, mittens are added. Warm hat covers her rooted Saran hair.

Angel Face FLEECE BUNTING.

Gabardine Bunting

5116, 16″ — $5.98
5119, 19″ — $7.98
5122, 22″ — $8.98
5125, 25″ — $9.98

Here's Angel Face, with painted hair, in a solid gabardine bunting that any little mother will love. Bright floral pattern across front and sleeves, which button up into mittens. Bunting zips up for comfort. Matching hat.

Angel Face GABARDINE BUNTING. This doll has molded, painted hair.

16″ Sun suit

5616 — $7.98

Angel Face has painted hair beneath the lacy baby bonnet. All dressed in a sun suit printed with tiny bear figures. Angel Face carries a bottle, for here she's a drink-and-wet doll.

Angel Face SUN SUIT. Molded hair doll.

21″ ANGEL FACE. Bright auburn hair and blue eyes. All original, with her wrist tag.
Carol J. Lindeman Collection.

ANGEL FACE DOLLS

All vinyl baby doll that is fully jointed at elbows, knees, shoulders and thighs. Drinks and actually wets when fed from plastic bottle attached. Dressed in all nylon dress with embroidered front panel, plastic covered diaper, matching maize or pink taffeta slip and bonnet. Height, 20 inches. Weight per shipping carton, 47 lbs.

ST-46-2093 ———————————————— Each $14.00
Twelve in a shipping carton.

20" ANGEL FACE. This one has extra joints at the knees and elbows. 1959 Geo. Worthington Co. Wholesale Catalog.

22" ANGEL FACE. Marked Arranbee. Vinyl head, rooted brunette hair. Vinyl limbs on pink oilcloth torso (variation of the all vinyl version). Mouth has molded tongue and two inset teeth. Original clothes; shoes and socks replaced. $95.00.

17" ANGEL FACE. Marked Arranbee. Organdy dress and bonnet are original.

21" ANGEL FACE. This one has a different hair style. Yellow organdy dress and slip are original. Yellow shoes and socks are replaced. $89.00.

Closeup showing cute turned-up nose.

21" ANGEL FACE. All vinyl, with jointed head and shoulders; legs are part of torso. but bend so she can sit properly. Molded open mouth with tongue, but no teeth. She is marked R&B and 19BBS. Suitable vintage dress. $55.00.

Closeup of 21" ANGEL FACE.

25" ANGEL FACE. All vinyl, marked R&B and 22BBS. Jointed neck and shoulders, flexible hips. Rooted hair. Snowsuit has separate hood and mittens. $75.00.

ANGEL FACE BABY DOLLS

Full jointed, all vinyl doll that drinks and wets. Dressed in romper and removable buttoned overshirt in azure blue or petal pink. Sun bonnet, sandals and plastic bottle attached. Height, 20 inches. Weight per shipping carton, 47 lbs.

ST-46-2001 .... Each $9.00

Twelve in a shipping carton.

20" ANGEL FACE. Drink and wet baby with molded hair. 1959 Geo. Worthington Co. Wholesale Catalog.

25" ANGEL FACE. 1959 Geo. Worthington Co. Wholesale Catalog.

ANGEL FACE BABY

An all vinyl drink and wet doll with five piece jointed body, and rooted hair wig. Dressed in organdy dress, lace trimmed neck, waist and pocket. Flowered pocket and flowered panel above waist. Straw hat with matching bow, taffeta slip, matching shoes and socks. Bottle attached. Height 25 inches

ST-46-2566 .... Each $13.00

Twelve in a shipping carton.

ANGEL FACE BABY

All vinyl drink and wet doll with five piece jointed body. Dressed in white nylon, lace trim with panel of pink and white nylon, ribbon trimmed around waist, shoulders and skirt. Matching lace trimmed bonnet and bow and matching taffeta slip, shoes and socks. Plastic bottle attached. Height 25 inches.

ST-46-2555 .... Each $11.00

Twelve in a shipping carton.

1959 Geo. Worthington Co. Wholesale Catalog.

ANGEL FACE BABY

An all vinyl drink and wet doll with five piece fully jointed body, and rooted hair. Dressed in pink nylon dress with pink figured nylon apron to match. Lace sleeves, matching taffeta slip, bonnet with bow to match shoes and socks. Plastic bottle attached. Height 16 inches.

ST-46-1662 .... Each $6.00

Twelve in a shipping carton.

1959 Geo. Worthington Co. Wholesale Catalog.

Vinyl arms, legs and head, moving eyes, mama voice, dynel hair. 24" high, choice of styles. *Not sold through jobbers.*

WALKS RIGHT OUT OF STOCK

Nancy

SHE WALKS, SAYS MAMA, HAS DYNEL HAIR

No mechanism to break or get out of order. When Nancy is held by the hands, she steps right along with her little mother. Speaks right up and says "MAMA". Her dynel hair can be washed, waved, combed and set. Her clothes are patterned after the ones her little mother wears. This modern type of walking doll, approved for lasting play value, is low priced, an outstanding feature item on which to base promotions.

July 1951 advertisement for Nancy in Playthings.

22" NANCY. Vinyl head marked Arranbee; vinyl limbs on cloth torso. Glued-on brunette wig of Dynel. Original pink check taffeta dress (may be missing a pinafore) and shoes. Wrist tag reads, "Nancy - Walks - Says Mama." The wrist booklet shows how to curl her hair with the attached curlers. $85.00.

Wrist booklet on 22" NANCY, both sides.

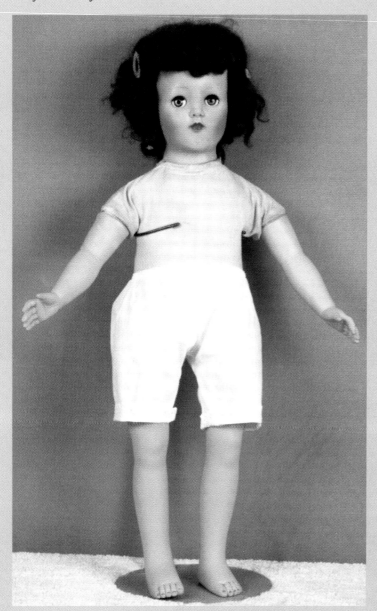

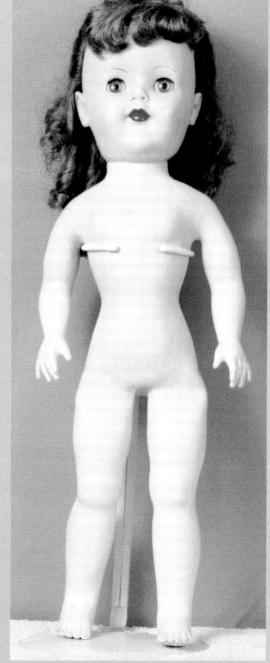

*Body construction of 22" NANCY.
Shorts are not original.*

26" GIRL. Marked R&B and 26VH. One piece body construction with flexible hips. Molded open/closed mouth and rooted hair. This may possibly be "Mother's Little Helper," advertised in 1954.

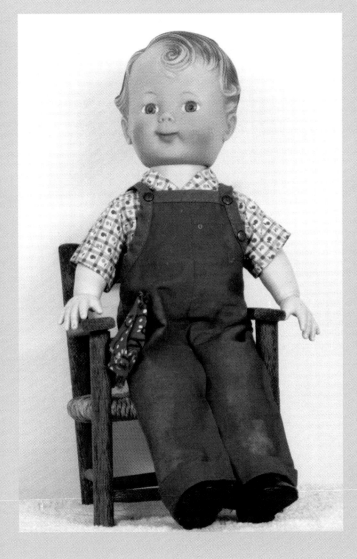

13" NEW BOY DOLL. Marked Arranbee. Vinyl head on one-piece latex body with flexible hips. Inset gray-blue eyes. Overalls and shirt belong to composition Nancy. Advertised in the June 1952 issue of Play-things, he came in sizes 12" to 17" and was promoted as a doll for boys to play with. Larger sizes had sleeping eyes. Note: New Boy Doll is actual name as it appeared in the ad. $45.00.

NEW BOY DOLL head. Marked Arranbee. The deeply-molded hair is the same as the preceding boy, but this one has sleeping eyes.

ANGEL SKIN TWINS

14" tall — $2.98 each

Brother and sister baby twins, each with a mischievous smile, made with washable latex body and vinyl head. Equipped with baby voice and glassine eyes. A real value at only $2.98 each.

ANGEL SKIN TWINS advertisement. 1955 R&B brochure.

8114 — $2.98

The Angel Skin Twins come dressed in matching button-up animal-print buntings Sleeves button into mittens.

8214 — $2.98

Pictures and description of ANGEL SKIN TWINS.

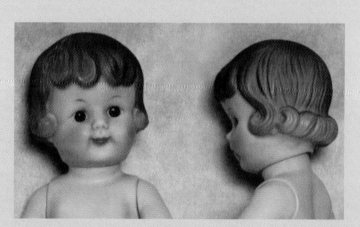

13" ANGEL SKIN SISTER. Vinyl head with deeply molded curls and set eyes. Her head is marked R&B. Body not original; she should have the same body as the boy.

Body construction of 13" ANGEL SKIN BROTHER. He is marked Arranbee.

NANCY TEEN AGE DOLL

All vinyl girl doll with five piece jointed body and rooted bobbed hair. Dressed in striped pink cotton outfit with belt and rhinestones and lace front. Navy blue faille coat, deep cuffs, new style wide white pique collar, lily of the valley spray at neck, rhinestone bracelet, pink felt hat with blue gros-grain ribbon, and low heeled simulated patent leather shoes. Height 16 inches.

ST-46-1693 _____ Each $8.00

Twelve in a shipping carton.

16" NANCY TEEN AGE DOLL. 1959 Geo. Worthington Co. Wholesale Catalog.

NANCY TEEN AGE DOLL

All vinyl girl doll with five piece jointed body. Rooted hair swept back in sophisticated hair do. Dressed in full skirted pink dress with lace collar worn under pink and white checked pinafore. Has apple pocket, wrist watch and low heeled shoes. Satin hair ribbon. Height, 16 inches.

ST-46-1691 _____ Each $7.00

Twelve in a shipping carton.

16" NANCY TEEN AGE DOLL. 1959 Geo. Worthington Co. Wholesale Catalog.

DREAM BABY

DREAM BABY — Here is a real "DREAM BABY" who has "just arrived". DREAM BABY, a newly-born infant, is just as life-like as she can be. All washable latex body, with soft vinyl head — amazingly realistic with sleeping eyes and a soft coo voice.

DREAM BABY advertisement. 1955 R&B brochure.

DREAM BABY — exactly as she looks when Mother brings her home from the hospital, wrapped securely in receiving blanket, tied with big ribbon, and wearing all undergarments necessary for her start in life.

17" Receiving Blanket
4117 — $4.98

22" Receiving Blanket
4122 — $8.98

Description of DREAM BABY in the 1955 brochure.

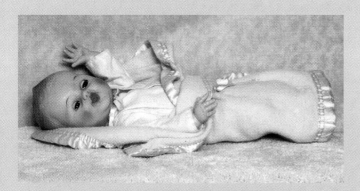

19" DREAM BABY. Unmarked. Vinyl, with fully jointed baby body. Molded light brown hair has a molded peak. Sleeping eyes. Original white flannel robe and diaper; pink fleece blanket. $135.00.

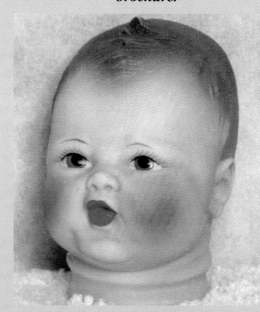

DREAM BABY. Vinyl head marked Arranbee. This one has painted eyes.

MY ANGEL WITH PINAFORE

All vinyl toddler doll with five piece all jointed body. With rooted hair wig. Dressed in a French blue pin dot cotton dress with organdy pinafore, socks and shoes. Height 25 inches.

ST-46-2514 .... Each $11.00
Twelve in a shipping carton.

25" MY ANGEL. 1959 Geo. Worthington Co.
Wholesale Catalog.

MY ANGEL IN SCHOOL PINAFORE

All jointed toddler doll with five piece body and rooted hair wig. Dressed in red dress and white pinafore with school house imprinted on it, red matching straw hat, red shoes and white socks. Height 25 inches.

ST-46-2523 .... Each $12.00
Twelve in a shipping carton.

25" MY ANGEL. 1959 Geo. Worthington Co.
Wholesale Catalog.

MY ANGEL IN POLO COAT

A five piece all jointed toddler doll with brown rooted hair in buster brown hair style. Dressed in red polished cotton dress wearing a tan camel hair colored polo coat, double breasted with half belt, nautical brass buttons. Coat is fully lined with plaid lining. Matching shoes and socks and white scarf tied around the head. Height 25 inches.

ST-46-2525 .... Each $14.00
Twelve in a shipping carton.

25" MY ANGEL. 1959 Geo. Worthington Co.
Wholesale Catalog.

Vinyl Novelties

The Arranbee Doll Company made other vinyl novelties during the 1950s. In the company's January 1951 *Playthings* advertisement, several Easter novelties were introduced. Jack Rabbit was an Easter Bunny with a vinyl head and stuffed cloth body; without an actual example, we assume that this was not a doll, but rather a stuffed toy, a not uncommon departure from dolls for Arranbee (a good example is the children's muff with a doll's head, made in the 1940s). In its February 1951 advertisement, Jack Rabbit was not mentioned; instead, Bootsie Rabbit appeared.

Another Easter item shown in the same advertisement is Bootsie Bunny. This was actually a vinyl baby doll in a bunting. The bonnet that came on the doll had rabbit ears, so it could be removed after Easter had passed. Unfortunately, once the bonnet was removed, it often got lost, and this baby appears today without this significant identification.

A curiosity of the January, 1951 advertisement is the mention of Peepers, described as "a beautiful new baby doll with vinyl head and moving eyes - ready soon!" Evidently, Arranbee either never produced this doll, or else changed its name; no example has been found, nor did subsequent advertisements mention her. It is possible that her new name was New Dream Baby, as advertised in March of 1951.

February 1951 advertisement in* Playthings *showing other vinyl Arranbee dolls promoted that year. Note that Baby Bunting Twins and Bootsie Bunny are described as having the same body construction as Angel Skin Twins. The Baby Bunting head is marked BBS R&B, with a size number.

When William Rothstein died in November of 1957, he left behind nearly forty years of outstanding dolls. Several members of his family carried on the business, with his widow, Rose, as advisor. In March of 1958, only a few short months after Mr. Rothstein death, Arranbee celebrated its 40th year, but few new models were added to its line of dolls. Later in the same year, the company became a division of Vogue Dolls, who then occupied the Fifth Avenue showroom with Arranbee as a division, and used the Arranbee molds until 1963.

Arranbee's association with Vogue spanned several decades; Vogue's earliest Toddles doll was actually an Arranbee doll. Appearing in 1937, this small, 7" – 8" doll was marked R&B Doll Co. on its back. By 1942, Vogue began producing its Toddles with only the "Doll Co." remaining on the back. Vogue added its own name to the head by 1943, and by 1944, all references to the R&B logo were gone. The bent baby leg version of this doll appeared as Vogue's Sunshine Baby, with "Vogue" on the head, and "Doll Co." on the back. Arranbee used this baby doll for its Ink-U-Bator Baby, and for a set of quints which had either straight legs or bent baby legs. These quints are often found as individual dolls today, with no reference to their original presentation. Several individual ones were produced as Dream Babies.

During the 1940's, Vogue produced a line of slim girl dolls in various sports outfits. Known as the Sportswomen Series, these unmarked composition dolls bear a striking resemblance to the all-composition Debu'teen dolls, both in facial features and clothing design. Since Vogue purchased these dolls as blanks and dressed them, they may possibly have come from Arranbee, especially since they were introduced after the 1938 debut of Debu'teen. As a result, the two dolls are often confused. However, the Debu'teen usually carries R&B on the back of its head.

Another Vogue doll that may possibly have come from Arranbee was the WAAC-ette doll of 1943-44. Otherwise unmarked, she has a faint A R on her back, which may be an incomplete blotting out of Arranbee.

Many of the R&B/Vogue vinyl dolls are unmarked or carry a number on the back, such as 63, but it is unknown if this numbering designated a mold number or the year of production. As with other unmarked dolls, only an original tag or box can identify one of these dolls.

An interesting example of the Arranbee/Vogue association is the Brikette doll. Vogue had obtained a license to copy this doll from Ferruccio Bonomi of Milan, Italy. The patent was obtained on June 7, 1960, for a term of 14 years. The patent, D-188-118, covered the design of the head, with a reference note to the *"Ideal Novelty and Toy Catalog*, 1948, page A-17, Teena, upper left". Originally, the patent was filed on August 31, 1959, but was then temporarily abandoned. The Teena doll does not appear in the two volume set *Collector's Guide to Ideal Dolls* by Judith Izen, so this reference is a mystery.

15" ANGEL BABY. Early 1960s vinyl baby marked only 63. Light brown molded hair, blue sleeping eyes, nursing mouth has hole for nipple. Doll wears flannel shirt, diaper, and original pink nylon snowsuit with attached mittens and feet. Baby bottle is tied to her wrist. Wrist tag says she is an "R&B Doll by the Arranbee Doll Company Division of Vogue Dolls of Medford, Mass." $85.00.

Closeup of face of 15"
ANGEL BABY.

Side view of 15" ANGEL BABY.

21" MY ANGEL. *Rigid and soft vinyl child having rooted hair. Flocked nylon dress is lined in pastel green. Her wrist tag reads, "R&B, Div. of Vogue Dolls." Never played with, in original box. $110.00. Marked P in a circle, like Coty Girl.*

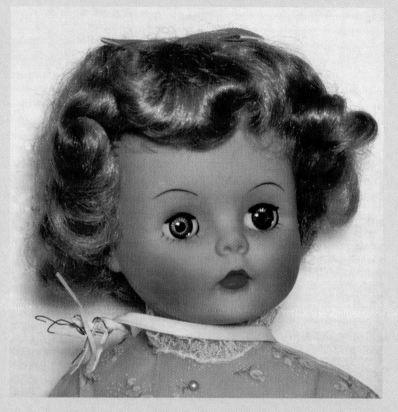

Facial features of 21" MY ANGEL. This doll came is several sizes up to 36". She came in a variety of dresses and was also available with a Dutch bob.

Box for 21" MY ANGEL.

15" ANGEL FACE. *Unmarked vinyl baby was one of the last dolls to bear the R&B name as part of Vogue Doll Company. She has rooted hair and sleeping eyes, and is all original, wearing a nylon dress and matching bonnet. Original tag and display box. The doll has a factory error in that her right arm is not exactly like her left one — evidently a substitute for a shorted production run of the correct one. $89.00.*

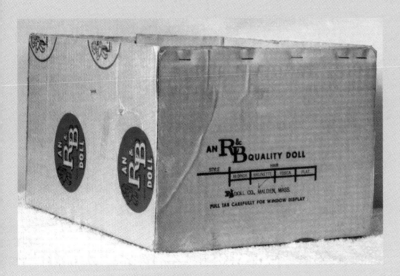

Box for 15" ANGEL FACE.

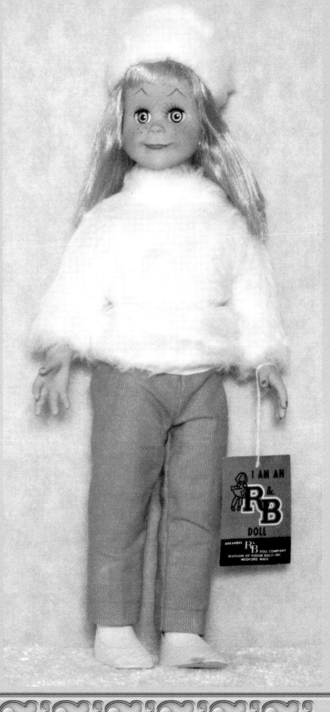

BRIKETTE. *Marked Vogue, copyright 1960. All vinyl character has an extra joint at the waist. Lustrous, carrot-colored rooted hair, emerald green eyes, and freckles. Original outfit consists of a fleece jacket, turquoise corduroy pants, white suede slip-on shoes. R&B/Vogue wrist tag.*
Dorothy Feingold Collection.

Facial features of 16" BRIKETTE. Note the unusually shaped eyebrows and the lashes painted to the upper outside edges only.

Profile of 16" BRIKETTE.

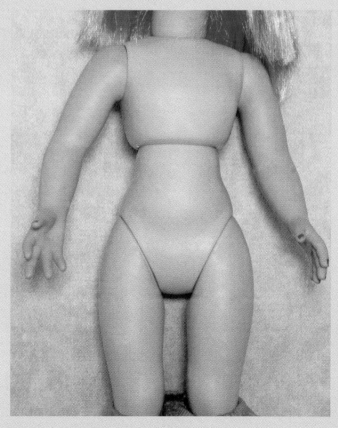

Body construction of 16" BRIKETTE.

Wrist tag on 16" Brikette.

I'M BRIKETTE

I'm a

. . . flirty emerald-eyed pixie.

. . . Sassy freckled-faced Show off

. . . frantic-antic tomboy

U. S. PATENT NO. D-188,118

Reverse side of Brikette wrist tag, with the U.S. Patent number stamped in red.

Paris Fair advertisement for Brikette showing her in the same outfit as the preceding doll.

EVERYTHING in DOLLS for 1960

The Ginny Doll Family

Fashion Leaders in Doll Society

AND

THE FAMOUS ARRANBEE DOLL LINE

Baby Dolls, Toddlers and Girl Dolls in a wide selection of sizes

Vogue Dolls INC.

Showrooms:
ROOM 656, 200 FIFTH AVE., N.Y., N.Y.

AN R&B DOLL

The combined Vogue/Arranbee advertisement in Playthings, March 1960 — the last advertisement in this magazine showing the R&B logo.

As with many doll companies, Arranbee purchased nude dolls from other manufacturers. Both composition and hard plastic dolls were acquired, hence the similarities in faces and bodies. Many known examples of this tradition exists and can be readily identified by the markings on the doll. However, there are a number of other dolls that bear no markings but have been attributed to Arranbee, either because of certain characteristics or other criteria.

An unusual hard plastic girl introduced in 1952 was Judy. She came in 15" and 19" sizes and had a metal knob on the side of her head, hidden in the braid. This metal knob was used to raise and lower the back section of the hair, hence the term "grow-hair." Unlike the Nanette and Nancy Lee dolls, she has an open mouth. Her face is similar to Horsman's "Cindy," and was perhaps made by that company. The doll is marked either 170 Made in USA, or 210, and both markings have a red stamp reading, "Pat. 2,537,536 [frequently unclear] and Other Pats. Pending." The patent was filed by Vera D. Lilienstern of Scarsdale, New York, in December of 1948, and received in January of 1951. There is no assignment, so apparently Ms. Lilienstern worked independently. The 15" doll was also stamped RDEC 2 in red, on the back of the torso neck. An ad in a 1952 Gimbels catalog shows her available only in a flannel nightgown, with no attribution to Arranbee. Several general doll books have attributed this doll to Arranbee, but research into original advertisements failed to confirm this identification and is made all the more difficult because other hard plastic dolls appear with either 210 or 170.

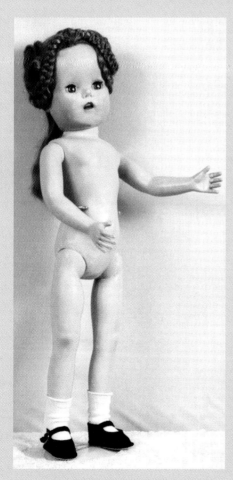

19" JUDY. Marked 170 Made in USA. Doll is well worn, but gives a good example of the growing hair mechanism. The hair is braided to hide the metal knob that raises and lowers the hair.

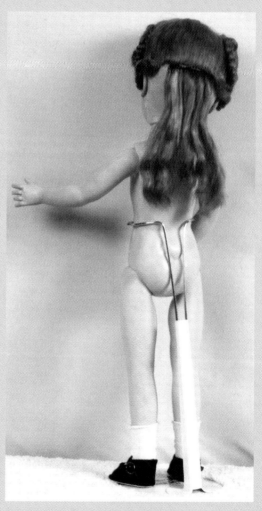

19" JUDY. Back view showing the hair at full length.

This side view of 19" JUDY shows the location of the metal knob. The curl just to the right of the knob has been pulled back to reveal the location of the knob. The patent number (in red) is just visible underneath her right arm.

15" JUDY. Strung hard plastic doll, marked Made in USA 170 on her back. The same patent number as the preceding doll is stamped in red on her side, with RDEC2 stamped on her neck. It is unknown just what her original clothing consisted of; the only advertisement found (Gimbel's mail order catalog) shows her wearing only a nightgown. The Nancy Lee vinyl toddler appears on the same page in that catalog. $85.00.

Closeup of 15" JUDY.

18" HARD PLASTIC WALKER. Vinyl head is marked with a c in a circle. Her face bears a striking similarity to the vinyl headed Nanette in Chapter 8. She is all original in a blue gown which has Arranbee characteristics. $185.00.

19" WALKER. Pin-jointed walker doll is marked only 210. This doll has been attributed to Arranbee, but the 210 number has been found on other companies' dolls. Note the similarity in the faces between this doll and the 15" Judy.

Facial features of 18" HARD PLASTIC WALKER.

20" MAMA DOLL. Composition swivel shoulder head, cloth torso, composition limbs. Head is faintly marked with a plus mark in a circle. Doll has metal eyes, an open mouth showing teeth, and a human hair wig. Face and clothing detail are all Arranbee characteristics, but she has not been positively identified as an Arranbee doll. She strikingly resembles the Nannette "Walk Talk" Mama doll in Chapter 7.

14" WW II NURSE. Unmarked composition girl shows definite resemblance to Debu'teen. She has metal eyes and closed mouth. $400.00 MIB, 1993.

11 14" NURSE in display box with extra clothing. The clothes are still attached to the cardboard insert and the doll removed only to photograph. She is in exceptional condition for a doll 60 or more years old. $400.00, 1993.

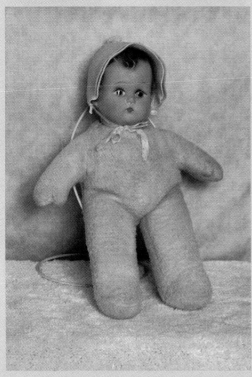

15" SNUGGLE DOLL. Unmarked composition head with painted features. Pink plush stuffed cloth body and removable pink bonnet. Arranbee advertised a Snuggle Doll in the 1930s, but without an original picture, this doll cannot be positively attributed to Arranbee.

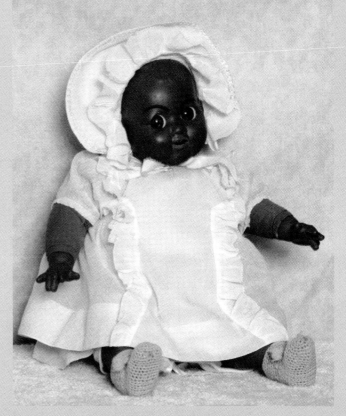

18" BISQUE BABY. Head is marked Germany Arranbee. A reproduction doll, she has set, side-glancing glass eyes. Her limbs are also made of bisque, on a fat cloth torso. She appears to be a copy of an original Arranbee doll, which has not been found. $135.00.

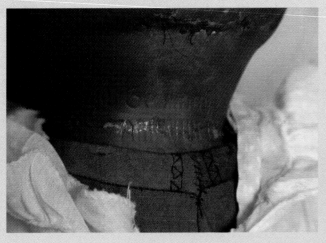

Closeup of preceding doll showing markings.

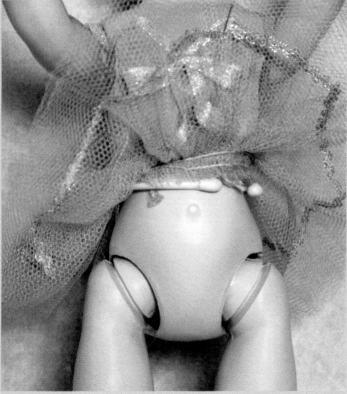

16" BALLERINAS. These two dolls are almost exactly alike, both in material and appearance, but with very marked differences. Both heads resemble some of the vinyl headed Nanette dolls; however, these two dolls are marked B16VW, with the left doll having an additional B after the W. The doll on the left has brush lashes, while the right one has molded lashes. The quality of material in the left doll's outfit is also more substantial and the skirt is fuller, with an additional underskirt. It would appear that both were made by the Valentine Doll Company, with one of them dressed by another company. In addition to being a more expensive doll overall, the left one's tutu also has a typical Arranbee characteristic, namely, two square snaps in the back.

Walking mechanism on the two ballerinas. Although typically a Valentine feature, other makers' dolls have been found with this particular mechanism, as well as with the well-formed, muscular legs.

Following is a list of doll trademarks registered by Arranbee.

Sources:

United States Government Patent Office, Directory of U.S. Doll Trademarks, 1888-1968, by Luella Tilton Hart, 1968.

Dictionary of Doll Marks, by Jean Bach, 1990.

1925	April 21	213,057	My Dream Baby
1930	March 17	297,403	Nancy and Kurly Head
1931	September 8	307,914	Class 22 - no name given
1934	August 30	355,559	Nanette
1938	October 24	411,983	Debu'teen
No date or number			*Cherrie Historical Portrait Dolls*
1939	February	21365,139	Class 22 - no name given
1940	June 20	433,208	Little Angel
1949	April 12	442,465	Class 22, dolls
1950	June 20	576,386	Unknown
1951	December 1	677,541	Nanette
1954	March 30	663,554	Taffy
	June 29	669,074	Littlest Angel, R&B
	July 6	669,391	Rock-Me Baby
1956	May 31	9,328	The Surprise Doll, a Littlest Angel Doll
1956	March 15	4,604	Sweet Pea
1957	December 13	40,544	April Showers

PATENTS

The following are some of the patents issued to Arranbee:

Simon & Halbig/Arranbee, Pt #74720. (A German patent number?)

My Dream Baby – US patent #202,243. Issued in 1925.

Drink n' Babe – US patent #1,595,840, dated August 10, 1926, for a special doll bottle with disappearing milk so that it appears as if the baby doll is really drinking her milk.

Dream Baby, US Patent #1,746,568. Issued in 1927.

"Sleeping Eyes for Rubber Doll" assigned US Patent #1,652,777, December 13, 1927, to Geisler, August, Limburg-on-the-Lake, Germany, assignor to Arranbee Doll Company.

An old Arranbee advertisement in 1929 stated that a US patent had been obtained for moveable joints, but no such patent was found.

"Doll with Baby Bottle," assigned US Patent #1,746,568 on February 11, 1930, was a different mechanism than the one patented in 1926. The patent was issued to Wallach, Leon, Brooklyn, assignor to W. and M. Rothstein and J. Ardbaum, Brooklyn, co-partners doing business as Arranbee Doll Co., New York, N.Y.

Miss International - Composition marked Design/Pat. Pend. No date given.

"Slow-closing doll's eye assembly." Kirby, Virgil D., to Arranbee Doll Co., Inc., Patent #2,813,372, issued November 19, 1957.

The patent for the Judy doll is included here, but the 1948 US Patent #2,537,536, stamped in red on the doll's torso, for a "grow-hair" feature does not mention Arranbee at all, only the designer, Vera D. Lilienstern. Also, the description does not mention the metal knob on the right side of the doll's head or any other mechanical device for raising and lowering the hair. A further puzzling note about this patent is that one of the other patent references cited names Rudolph Hopf for a 1927 patent assigned to Averill. This Hopf is evidently a relative of Ruby Hopf, Arranbee's head designer, but no further relationship can be inferred at this time.

The reader should be aware that some of the dolls listed below were found in other general doll books and magazines, but have not been verified by the authors as being Arranbee dolls. It may be that a name given to a doll by its original owner was carried with the doll, with its original name forgotten, and therefore, lost to history. Since Arranbee produced many dolls both for itself and for other doll companies, it would be nearly impossible to name all of them.

15" Composition and cloth. Early 1930's doll made by Arranbee for its employees. Torso is a stamped Central Bag Co. stuffed with excelsior.

15" Army Girl. Painted eyes, painted molded hair. Wearing khaki colored army suit and cap. This appears to be the same model as the preceding doll.

19" Rosie. Composition and cloth marked Arranbee. A Nancy-type doll.

21" Nancy Jean. All composition marked R&B. Resembles Debu'teen and may be one of the Teen series such as Rosalie.

14" Bessie Toddler. All composition black doll, similar to Dream Baby. Painted side-glancing eyes, molded hair with 3 tufts, dimples. Marked R&B on the head.

14" Snuggle Muff. 1940 composition head with R&B on front neck, painted eyes on child's plush muff.

16" Snuggle Doll, 1942 composition head marked R&B, molded brown hair or wig and stuffed cord or plush body.

15" Happytime. Composition and cloth, marked R&B/250. Mohair wig over molded hair; closed mouth.

14" Champ. Composition Dream Baby toddler doll in purple satin boxing outfit with Champ printed on jacket back and boxing shorts. Realistic leather boxing gloves.

17" Snuggle Doll. 1941 composition head (no marks), blond wig, inset blue eyes. Cord stuffed body with matching, removable bonnet.

17" Gloria Jean. All composition, with vivid blue eyes. Gloria Jean was a child actress who played a 12-year-old singer in the 1940 movie *A Little Bit of Heaven*. Face has both Debu'teen and Nancy Lee facial characteristics.

17" Little Miss Movie. A competitor to Shirley Temple.

21" So Big. Composition and cloth baby doll marked R&B.

14" Baby Kaye. Composition and cloth baby doll with open/closed mouth. Marked R&B.

15" Happy Time. Transition doll having a hard plastic head marked R&B 250 and composition limbs on a stuffed cloth torso.

18" Darling Daisy Bride. Hard plastic girl. Gown label states her name.

14" Nanette Cowgirl. 1954, marked R&B.

18" Angeline. Hard plastic, with mohair wig, wearing a gold skating dress. Ca 1951 – 52.

14" Francine. Hard plastic girl with waist length wig. Ca. 1955. Also in 18" size.

12" Dream Baby. 1954 hard plastic toddler reissued from original composition mold.

36" My Angel Walking Doll. Polyethylene body and legs; soft vinyl head and arms. Vogue later used this doll for Walking Ginny.

12" Sweet Angel. 1957 vinyl baby, marked R&B. Issued as Little Dear in 1959.

8" Baby Marie. All vinyl baby doll in a Woolworth box, 1960.

15" Susan. This appears to be the same doll as the Nancy Lee vinyl toddler, but having long hair.

Bibliography

Arranbee Doll Company, various brochures, advertisements, and articles.

Blue Book of Doll Values, I – 15, Jan Foulke, Hobby House Press.

Buyers Directory of American Toys for 1929, published by Toys & Novelties.

Collectors Encyclopedia of American Composition Dolls, 1999, Ursula R. Mertz. Collector Books.

Collector's Encyclopedia of Vogue Dolls. Judith Izen and Carol Stover, 1998. Collector Books.

Collector's Guide to Ideal Dolls, vol. II. Judith Izen, 1999, Collector Books.

Directory of U.S. Doll Trademarks, 1888 – 1968, Luella Tilton Hart, 1968.

Antique Trader's Doll Makers & Marks, Dawn Herlocher, 1999. Antique Trader Books.

Dolls and Accessories of the 1950's, 1998. Dian Zillner, Schiffer Publishing, Ltd.

Glamour Dolls of the 1950's and 1960s, 1988, Polly and Pam Judd, Hobby House Press.

Hard Plastic Dolls — Identification & Price Guide, I & II, Polly and Pam Judd, Hobby House Press.

Lush and Lovely...R&B Dolls, Margaret Groninger & Anne Schwarz, August/September 1982 Doll Reader Magazine.

Modern Collectors Dolls, I-VIII, Patricia Smith. Collector Books.

Modern Collectors Dolls, I-IV, Patsy Moyer. Collector Books.

More Twentieth Century Dolls, Vol. I, 1974, Johana Gast Anderton. Wallace-Homestead Book Co.

Playthings, 1920 through 1960.

The Standard Modern Doll – Identification & Value Guide. Bill Schroeder, 1979. Collector Books.